Grace Is Not A Blue-Eyed Blonde

Grace is the Joyous Unmerited Blessing of God

by
Dr. Eugene C. Rollins

authorHOUSE®

AuthorHouse™
1663 Liberty Drive, Suite 200
Bloomington, IN 47403
www.authorhouse.com
Phone: 1-800-839-8640

First published by AuthorHouse   11/12/2008

ISBN: 978-1-4389-2790-9 (sc)

Library of Congress Control Number: 2008909971

Printed in the United States of America
Bloomington, Indiana

This book is printed on acid-free paper.

❦ *Dedication* ❧

Grace comes in many forms. In my life, grace has come as "a blue-eyed blonde." I dedicate this work to my "blue-eyed blonde" wife, Linda. She has been a major source of grace for me over the past twenty-three years. Her honest, unconditional criticism of my sermons has been hurtful and helpful but always graceful.

❦ Grace ❧

After centuries of handling and mishandling, most religious words have become so shopworn that nobody's much interested anymore. Not so with *grace*, for some reason. Mysteriously, even derivatives like *gracious* and *graceful* still have some of the bloom left.

Grace is something you can never get but only be given. There's no way to earn it or deserve it or bring it about, any more than you can deserve the taste of raspberries and cream or earn good looks or bring about your own birth.

A good sleep is grace and so are good dreams. Most tears are grace. The smell of rain is grace. Somebody loving you is grace. Loving somebody is grace. Have you ever *tried* to love somebody?

A crucial eccentricity of the Christian faith is the assertion that people are saved by grace. There's nothing you *have* to do. There's nothing you have to *do*.

The grace of God means something like: Here is your life. You might never have been, but you are because the party wouldn't have been complete without you. Here is the world. Beautiful and terrible things will happen. Don't be afraid. I am with you. Nothing can ever separate us. It's for you that I created the universe. I love you.

There's only one catch. Like any other gift, the gift of grace can be yours only if you'll reach out and take it.

Maybe being able to reach out and take it is a gift too.

From *Listening to Your Life: Daily Meditations with Frederick Buechner,* compiled by George Connor, San Francisco: Harper, 1992, pp. 288–289.

❧ *Foreword* ❧

One of the most unappetizing features of many preachers is their gaudy confidence that they possess absolute truth, and nothing but the truth, about God to the exclusion of every divergent theological concept. It is as though they are totally oblivious to the truth that the God question is too complex and great of mystery for there to be only one single approach to or understanding of it. Preachers of this ilk have no appreciation for Paul's observation that "now we see through a glass darkly"—that is to say, in things theological, certainly is illusion. As Paul said in I Timothy 1:7 about some who wanted to be teachers, "They do not know what they are talking about or what they do confidently affirm."

But, as demonstrated in this sermon series exploring the nature and depths of God's grace, the enlightened, courageously candid, open-minded, and open-armed ministry of Gene Rollins brings to the Liberty Hill community and its environs a splendidly joyful opportunity to appreciably augment its understanding of the not altogether understandable God question, particularly as that question relates to God's grace. I think I know the Reverend Dr. Rollins well enough to say that he believes in the pursuit of truth—not its attainment or its final definition, but its pursuit.

The American Declaration of Independence identifies "the pursuit of happiness" as a right given to us by God. Surely, the pursuit of truth is an integral part of that God-given right to pursue happiness. Even though reading about these searchings for the truth about God's grace is not as happy an experience as hearing them preached on the banks of Lake Wateree in the summertime, reading them is the next best thing.

Bruce Davis, Esquire

Mount Pleasant, SC

Contents

Chapter One

Origin of the Material

This material was first prepared as sermons and was delivered at Lakeside Worship on Wateree Lake in Kershaw County, South Carolina. Liberty Hill Presbyterian Church (PCUSA) began this outreach in July of 1977. These sermons were delivered in the summer of 2001.

Transcribing the spoken word into the written word has been the dream of Mrs. Sylvia Hudson for many years. For a number of years, Mrs. Hudson was the office manager at the church and is a past Elder. Had it not been for her dream, a dream that she doggedly would not let go, you would not be reading these words today.

For forty-plus years I have been amazed that anyone would come, sit, and listen to anything I had to say. Although amazed, the amazement did not lead me to believe that anyone would have any interest in reading what I had to say; therefore, it is fully to her credit that these spoken sermons now appear in print.

✍ *Chapter Two* ✍

The Sermon Syllabus

AN INTRODUCTION TO THE SERMON SYLLABUS

There are as many methods of sermon preparation as there are preachers. But for me, there is only one. I pastored a church for four years (1966–1970) before attending seminary. I preached three sermons each week without really knowing what I was doing. In my latter years I have prayed often for those persecuted people.

I went to Southwestern Baptist Theological Seminary in Fort Worth, Texas, in August of 1970. One of my first classes was H. C. Brown's preaching class entitled "Steps to the Sermon,"[1] and it changed my life. For the first time I saw a method in the madness of developing a sermon.

FINDING A TEXT

The Scripture text or an idea for a sermon comes from many sources. It may be a planned program of preaching such as the lectionary. The texts are developed on a three-year cycle, A, B, and C. A new year begins with the first Sunday of Advent. I always read the lectionary texts, but I do not feel obligated to preach them. The first source of a text for me is the experience of my church members, our community, and then our state, nation, and world. The question on my mind and heart is always, "What are their needs?" Having a sense of their need, I then look for a text, a parable, a story, or an experience within Scripture.

THE CENTRAL IDEA OF THE TEXT

The second task is determining the central idea within the text. The text must be considered within its context. That means the context of the paragraph, the book, the Bible itself, and the historical context of when and why it was written. I always keep in mind the principle of "progressive revelation," which means that the passage being interpreted is seen in the light of its relation to the stages of development of biblical peoples and writers. For example, their worldview was that the earth was in three levels: hell, earth, and heaven, being flat with four corners. A text must be understood from the prevailing worldview. In the pre-scientific world, people were less interested in what actually happened but were more concerned with what the event *meant.* In the historical context of the Bible, there evolved two ways of thinking, speaking, writing, and acquiring knowledge which scholars have defined as *mythos* and *logos.*[2] Mythos is primarily concerned with timeless truths: life's meaning and purpose. Mythological stories were not intended to be taken literally. They were the ancient forms of psychology and philosophy. For the truth of the myth to be told and perpetuated, it took the form of a story.

Logos is also a way of getting at the truth, but it deals with facts and external realities. Logos is practical and rational and would not attempt to deal with the ultimate values of life. Both mythos and logos are essential. They need each other! They are complementary methods of approaching truth. In the pre-scientific world, both were regarded as indispensable. But by the eighteenth century, the people of Europe and America had achieved so much in science and technology that they began to discount mythos as inessential false superstition. The fundamentalists, on the other hand, turned the mythos of their faith into logos, and the result is confusion in both camps.[3]

Along with mythos and logos, I keep *Midrash* in mind. Midrash is a Hebrew/Jewish way of saying that everything in the present must somehow be connected with a sacred experience in the past. Midrash is the retelling of a timeless truth so that the truth may be experienced afresh in each generation. It is the ability to rework an ancient theme or timeless truth into a new context.[4]

The above method has been called the *grammatico-historical* approach. I will study the Hebrew if it is an Old Testament text, or the Greek if it is in the New. I must know what the words mean. I ask, "What is the primary meaning of this word as it is used in Scripture?" The most common way to misinterpret the text is to isolate the meaning and/or context of the word.

Once the central idea of the text (CIT) is found, it is stated, or written in the syllabus, in the past tense. For example, the CIT of Genesis 3:8–13 and verse 21 is: "When Adam and Eve sinned and hid themselves in the garden, God came looking for them."

THE THESIS

The thesis is a restatement of the CIT but in a clear present-tense fashion. For example, the thesis of the above CIT would be, "God's grace pursues us even while we are hiding." The thesis statement is a brief declarative sentence of the central idea of the sermon. It should be the *key sentence* of the sermon. The thesis should create human interest with vitality and difference but yet be timeless and universal. It should be stated as a truth that is good for all time. I spend as much time with developing the thesis as I do discovering the CIT. The thesis of the sermon should be related to the objective of the sermon.

THE OBJECTIVE

The objective of the sermon I place under "purpose." There is a major objective and a specific objective. The purpose of the sermon should be to meet some basic need in the lives of the people. The major objective is determined by the needs of the people. I use five basic needs of the people: evangelistic, devotional, doctrinal, ethical/actional, and supportive. For example, the above thesis of "God's grace pursues us even while we are hiding" would be evangelistic.

The specific objective expresses a positive and affirmative statement, expressing the response from the congregation that I desire from this one particular sermon. The specific response coming from the above major objective would be "Through the power of the Holy Spirit, I hope to lead each of us in allowing God's grace to find us." I always begin that statement with "Through the power of the Holy Spirit . . ." I know that I cannot cause or create any response from my people, and I am also aware that it is not in my job description to do so. That is the job of the Holy Spirit. But I think the Holy Spirit can and does use the single clarity of the statement to teach and convict hearts. Next comes the title.

THE TITLE

A title, well stated and precisely phrased, helps the congregation to understand clearly the intent of the sermon. It helps the preacher to have a word picture of the whole body of the sermon. It will serve as a fence to keep the digressions out and a greater focus on the content. When you see a preacher or speaker without a title for what he or she is going to say, expect a rambling talk and you will not be disappointed.

The title should be clear! It is not a restatement of the thesis but it should be tied to or connected in some way. The thesis should not point south and the title point north. Both should carry the listener's thoughts in the same direction.

The title should be accurate! In the example sermon, it is the first sermon in a series of fourteen, and it is about grace. Therefore, the title is "Grace! It's Beginning." Sometimes the preacher will read a Scripture text and then nothing is said that remotely relates to what was read in the text. This is also true of titles. A printed title is there, but the idea or scope of it never comes up. The title is not a launching pad to go into the "wild blue yonder."

The title should be specific! In the example sermon, the emphasis is upon grace, but to just have the one word would be too general. I could have used "Grace Began in the Garden of Eden," but it is not as specific as the title "Grace! It's Beginning."

The title should be brief! A one-word title is most often too general in scope, but more than seven words is burdensome and will not be remembered by the preacher or the audience.

The title should be catchy but not cheap or sensational. In H. C. Brown's sermon class, we were told about a sermon on the Cross with the title "Death on a Stick." That is cheap, not catchy. The book *Steps to The Sermon* has the example of the Gadarenes man of Luke Chapter 8 with the title "A Nudist in a Graveyard"; or worse yet, a sermon on the death of John the Baptist with the title "The Baptist Preacher Who Lost His Head at a Dance."[5] These are vulgar and somewhat sexually suggestive. The introduction is next.

THE INTRODUCTION

I usually do not develop the introduction until after the body of the sermon and more often only after the conclusion. The introduction should prepare the way for the sermon body. The primary purpose is threefold: to arouse the interest of the audience, to highlight the purpose of the message, and to establish empathy between the speaker and the audience. The introduction is critically important to the outcome of the message.

If the introduction falls flat on its face, the sermon is not likely to recover. When that happens, move quickly to the conclusion and go home. My most used type of introduction is the illustration. I use a joke only when the joke relates to the title or the first point of the sermon.

THE OUTLINE

The outline is the body of the sermon. The body is broken up into smaller parts so it can be remembered by the speaker and the hearer. There is a joke about a sermon being "three points and a poem." That is not a bad definition of the sermon body. I most often use three points and rarely ever more than five. If you do not have more than one point, you do not have an outline.

THE CONCLUSION

The only thing more important to the sermon than the conclusion is the text. The conclusion in some way restates the thesis, revisits the purpose, or calls final attention to the title. The conclusion should not be rambling, wordy, or aimless. As a general rule it should be brief, clear, specific, positive, and personal. I try to limit my conclusion to no more than seven percent of the total sermon. The conclusion should answer the question, "What do you want me to do and how do you want me to do it?"

I have not prepared a sermon in thirty-five years without using the sermon syllabus method. In four of the five churches I have pastored over these forty-two years, I put a printed copy into the church bulletin for a while and then, without explanation, stopped having it in the bulletin. Without exception, a number of people asked for its return, sharing how it helped them "stay with the message" or "remember the message." It is for that reason and with that hope that I include it in this work. May it help you to stay with the message and to remember the message.

Chapter Three

Grace! It's Beginning

SERMON SERIES: "Grace Is Not a Blue-Eyed Blonde"

SERMON THEME: Grace is the joyous, unmerited blessing of God.

TEXT: Genesis 3:8–13, 21

CIT (central idea of the text): When Adam and Eve hid in the garden, God came looking for them.

THESIS: God's grace pursues us even while we are hiding.

PURPOSE: *Major objective:* evangelical

Specific objective: Through the power of the Holy Spirit, I hope to lead each of us in allowing God's grace to find us.

TITLE: "GRACE! IT'S BEGINNING"

INTRODUCTION

OUTLINE:

I.Grace Began in the Garden of Creation—v. 8

II.Grace Began in Pursuit—v. 9

III.Grace Began in Provision—v. 21

CONCLUSION

Dr. Eugene C. Rollins

Scripture Reading: Genesis 3:8–13, 21

Then the man and his wife heard the sound of the Lord God as he was walking in the garden in the cool of the day, and they hid from the Lord God among the trees of the garden. But the Lord God called to the man, "Where are you?"

He answered, "I heard you in the garden and I was afraid because I was naked; so I hid."

And he said, "Who told you that you were naked? Have you eaten from the tree that I commanded you not to eat from?"

The man said, "The woman you put here with me, she gave me some fruit from the tree, and I ate it."

Then the Lord God said to the woman, "What is this you have done?"

The woman said, "The serpent deceived me, and I ate."

The Lord God made garments of skin for Adam and his wife and clothed them.

Introduction

I've been taken a little bit by surprise. I have had time to work through the shock of it and sit with it for a little while and I realized more deeply what was taking place. I have already received more criticism about this series than I did on the series "The Parallel Teachings of Buddha and Jesus," and I've not even begun this one yet.

I was more than a little taken back when a person said to me, "The title is sacrilegious. 'Grace Is Not a Blue-eyed Blonde.' That's sacrilegious." Well, I was so taken aback by it that I didn't have an answer for it. But the more I thought about it I said, "That's true." And you know what else, "grace" IS sacrilegious. It is! And you're going to hear that from me this summer. I believe grace is the most unique, absolutely unique, gift of the Christian church. But it is one of the most misunderstood theological gifts of the Christian church.

This same person said to me, "You say on your sermon syllabus for June 24 that grace is ridiculous." Again I was so taken aback, I didn't quite know what to say. I didn't say anything. But you know what the truth is; it IS ridiculous. I am going to show you the ridiculous nature of it all through the Scriptures. It is absolutely ridiculous that a holy, righteous, and pure God would just forgive unrighteous, unholy, marred, scarred, wounded creature kind. It's ridiculous.

We were struggling this past week with what to put on the bulletin front. Well, I was already shell shocked, so I didn't want to put "Grace Is Not a Blue-Eyed Blonde" on there. I knew that much. So I wimped out and put the other one on there—a little safer. But you know what you're going to see on there? (My courage came back to me a little this week.) I don't care whether they shoot me or not. I've got another job!

You're going to see on the bulletin an acrostic GRACE: **G**od's **R**idiculous **A**ffirmation **C**oncerning **E**veryone. You know what you're going to accuse me of then? "You're a Universalist. You believe everybody's got grace and everybody's going to Heaven and all we have to do is announce it." So be it.

I remind myself of what the Bible says, "If you can't take the heat, then get out of the kitchen." No, I believe that was Harry Truman, wasn't it? But you know how we get things in life mixed up. Like "Cleanliness is next to Godliness," things like that.

I. Grace Began in the Garden of Creation

Grace has its beginning in the poetry of creation. You see, I was so shell shocked that I wimped out on that first point of the sermon. I took out "poetry."

A year and a half ago, I was doing a wedding in a garden scene and so I said, as I started the wedding, "In this beautiful garden that we are in this afternoon, it is appropriate that we go to the beauty of the mytho-poetic literature of Genesis." And I went right to the part about the Garden and talked about God joining Adam and Eve. During the wedding reception, this person comes up to me and meanders kind of close, invading my space a little bit. He said, "Mytho-poetic?"

"Yep."

"What does that mean?"

I said, "I understand it to mean that Genesis is a beautiful poem that has deep, abiding truth."

He said, "You don't believe it's real?"

I said, "If you mean real as literal, no. I don't believe it's literal."

He just turns to walk off and he says, "Ain't much of a preacher; don't even believe the Bible. You know, you either believe that the Genesis story is literal or you don't believe it at all."

Don't let people put you in a predicament of having this kind of philosophy or this kind of thinking. Don't let them do that. They do that to us all the time. For example, cats see in the dark. Midnight is a cat. Therefore, Midnight sees in the dark. Don't let people hem you in with that faulty kind of philosophy. You don't have to. You know why they named the cat Midnight? She was blind. So don't let people catch you in that kind of philosophy.

The poem in Genesis about God creating everything is absolutely beautiful and gorgeous. Do not allow the paranoid creationists to take that away from you. Do not get caught up in the dualism that you are either for Evolution or you are for the Creation story. Don't let them do that to you. Very few things in life are either this or that. That's the biggest problem that people come to me with.

A lady says to me, "I either have to stay in this horrible marriage or I have to leave it."

I say, "Oh no, there are other options."

She looks at me kind of funny and says, "Well, what? I either stay in this horrible marriage or I leave it."

I say, "No. You can take a contract out on him."

She stares at me in shock and says, "You mean have him murdered?"

I said, "Yeah. I hope you wouldn't do that, but that's an option, so we've already got three. You can leave him, you can stay, or you can have him murdered. Now let's work together and see if we can't find another one or two." And we always do. Don't let them put you in a box where you either believe in Evolution or you believe in Creation. You can believe in Evolution *and* you can believe in Creation.

Read the story a little more carefully. "In the beginning God created time. Twenty-four hours in a day, and then on the first day God created this." No, I believe God created the universe before WE ever created time, quite some time later. Again, don't let them put you in some kind of box.

Grace in the beginning was the beautiful poetry of creation. God creates for us this beautiful earth, and God creates it out of grace. You know some theologians say God was lonely and wanted a creature to share life with. And there are other theologians that say God is sovereign and that God can't be lonely. Well, let's not go there either. But if God was lonely and wanted a companion, He could have created a beautiful blue-eyed blonde and called her Grace. He, or She, did not have to create this and say I am also going to create you in my spiritual image so you can enjoy the beauty of creation. There's the beginning of grace. Grace in creation. This grace that creates is also a grace that pursues.

II. Grace Began in Pursuit

A pastor had a family visit his church, and the next week he called the family at home. A little voice answered the phone and said in a whisper, "Hello."

The pastor said, "Is your mother there?"

And the little voice again whispered, "She's busy."

The pastor said, "Well, is anyone else there? Is your father there?"

(Whispering) "Yes."

"Could I speak to him?"

13

(Whispering) "He's busy."

"Is there anyone else there?"

(Whispering) "Policemen."

"Policemen? Could I speak to one of them?"

(Whispering) "They're busy."

"Well, is there anyone else there?"

(Whispering) "Firemen."

"Firemen? Could I speak to one of them?"

(Whispering) "They're busy."

"Why is everyone so busy?"

(Whispering) "They're looking for me!"

Can't you just see that little five year old holding that cordless telephone hiding in the basement?

Out of grace, God creates human beings and puts them in a garden, and God comes back to the garden to fellowship with them in the cool of the day. They are not there. Notice the grace. "Where are you?" God knows where they are. God knows what's happened, but notice the grace. They are over there behind the trees in the bushes.

There they are behind the bushes. God knows what's happened. They are guilty, they're shameful, they're hiding. God knows why they're sinful, shameful, and hiding—because they sinned. They broke the one commandment that God gave them: "Do not eat of this tree." They ate of it. They feel guilty and shameful and are hiding. God's word said that the day they ate the fruit of that tree, they would die. The commandment's already been broken. There they are over there in the bushes behind the tree. All God has to do is run a little lightning out of the finger. Have you ever been around a tree when lightning hits? Better yet, have you ever been standing on a metal deer stand in a tree when lightning hits about forty yards away? Talk about grace. It's kind of like being on the golf course. If you're ever on the golf course when lightning strikes, pick up the two iron and hold it up. Even God can't hit a two iron.

All God had to do was to say, "You broke the law. The law says, 'You break it, you die.'" Zap! There they are. Fried. Little pretzels, behind that tree in the bush.

What does God do? "Adam, Eve. Where are you?" Notice the pursuit. Notice the grace. God does not just kill them.

"Where are you? Talk to me. Why are you hiding?"

"Well, I ate of the fruit. The woman you gave me gave me the fruit." Sin, shame, and guilt always blame.

The woman says, "The serpent you created and put in the garden deceived me and I ate." Sin, shame, guilt always blames.

Thank goodness we have the federal government, the state government, and spouses. We always have somebody to blame. If it doesn't fall into those categories, we can always go to the ultimate and blame God.

Sin. Shame. Guilt. Hiding. Blame.

Aren't you thankful God pursues us when we sin and hide? Sin always breaks the fellowship of God and we hide. We don't want to be found— that's part of us. But grace pursues. Grace hunts us out.

Years ago, I came home from a convention to find that we had a new guest in our house. My son, who was about fourteen at the time, had acquired a German shepherd dog. She had milk bags hanging down to the ground. She was supposedly on the police force and was being trained or something and had thirteen puppies. They disposed of the puppies and were going to dispose of her. Out of grace, my son brought her home. What in the world was I going to do with this dog? Lady— and I do not know why they named her that with her in that kind of condition—turned out to be one of the most beautiful gifts in my life. For seven years I ran with her for six days a week at Furman University. Every day. A magnificent dog. Lady had a habit. She would love to get in the outside trash cans and go through everything. The first time she did that, I scolded her verbally. The second time she did that, I got on her with the newspaper. Every day when I would roll into the drive, she would come around the house, tail wagging, waiting for me to open the door of the car. Except, that is, the days when she got into the trash. When I turned into the driveway, no Lady, no wagging tail, I knew the first thing I had to do before going into the house was to clean up the trash. Where was Lady? She found her hiding place under the house. She knew when she got into the trash, she had sinned, broken my law. She had sinned. I don't know how much fear she had that I was going to whale the daylights out of her.

We as humans move a little deeper but with the same instincts. When we sin, we hide. We feel guilty. We feel shame. We do not want to take the responsibility. On the one hand, we do not want God to find us; but on the other hand, we want God to find us. We miss the fellowship. We want to be reconciled. And the grace of God pursues us.

"Where are you?" When we fail to meet God in devotion, when we fail to meet God in prayer, when we fail to meet God in thought, when we are hiding. "Where are you? I've missed you. I'm here in the cool of the day to fellowship with you. Where are you? What's happened to you? Tell me about it."

God does not kill them. God pursues them and finds them. The Scripture says on the day you eat thereof, you'll die. And those who take the book literally say, "Well, what it meant was that he died in his soul." What it meant was he was going to die sometime. Oh, they want to take that part poetically but not take other parts poetically. Okay. Have it your way. Don't let them catch you in that trap.

The grace of God pursues and hunts out. Notice what grace in the beginning also does. It creates this marvelous universe and all the blessings we enjoy. Grace pursues us when we fail and sin and when we are willfully disobedient and hide. The grace of God pursues us, looks for us in the bushes, calls for us. Grace also provides.

III. Grace Began in Provision

Get this picture. Here's Adam and Eve and they have sinned and they look at each other and go, "Oh! We're naked. We've got to cover up." Shame. Guilt. So they use what's available. They pick some leaves off a fig bush. As I remember a fig bush, it has a pretty good size leaf, about the size of my hand. So they take this fig bush and this innate woman with a needle, and they sew these leaves together and make these little aprons. But here they are with this little garment of fig leaves to cover their nakedness. That probably happened in the morning. I don't know how long it takes fig leaves to dry but they go to bed. They turn over. Crinkle, crinkle, crinkle. They wake up in the morning. It's gone! Fallen off! They're naked again! You know what that is? Look at it carefully. That is a beautiful picture of works righteousness. That is the most graphic picture you'll ever see anywhere of works righteousness.

Save thyself. After you've sinned, fallen short, feel shameful, and are hiding, rightly relate yourself to God by doing good works. Do something. Give a tenth to the church. I appreciate it, but it's not going to help you. Send a Will. Send an endowment. We'll name something after you if it's big enough. We appreciate it but it's not going to help you.

You say, I'm going to keep all the commandments. I'm going to do good, be good. That's good and fine. I hope you do. I hope you don't steal, lie, cheat, shoot somebody. But it's not going to help you. That is works righteousness. That is fig leaves sewn together that will dry, crumple, and fall apart, and you will be as naked and as destitute as the moment you started sewing the green ones together.

Grace provides. Verse 21 says that God clothed Adam and Eve with skin. The first blood had to be shed. The first animal died in the need of humankind, and there they are presented with a sacrifice—that's my thoughts. It's not in Scripture. But they are presented with skin that will not break, crinkle, dry, or fall apart. That is grace. God pursued them in their nakedness and provided for them clothing. God, in God's grace, always pursues us.

The Scripture tells us that Jesus is walking the road to Jericho, and there is a little man that is hiding in a sycamore tree. Why is he hiding? He is a tax collector. He has cheated, robbed, taken what was not his. He is a traitor to his own cause. He is a Jew collecting taxes for the Roman government. He's hiding in the tree because he is shameful. Jesus stops under the tree, looks up, and says, "Zacchaeus, come down." Grace pursuing, Jesus goes to Zacchaeus' home and everybody is astonished.

"Look at him. He's going home with a sinner." Grace that pursues is ridiculous. We don't like it. It's scary.

"Surely, preacher, you can't tell everyone in your congregation that their life with God is a life with grace. Don't tell them that. Where's your salary coming from? Who's going to keep the church up?"

We've got to milk a little bit of the guilt gland. It's grace plus your good giving. "If you tell them it's just grace, there won't be anybody there to preach to."

Halleluiah, I won't have to do it anymore! I can fish, golf, hunt. It's grace and it is absolutely ridiculous.

Conclusion

You know the history of our country. There was a time when slavery was an institution. A young congressman went to a slave auction. There was a young black girl put up for auction. The congressman made a bid. Another person outbid him. The congressman made another bid. Another person outbid him. The congressman made another bid. No one outbid him. The auctioneer brought the slave girl to him and the congressman said, "Take her chains off." They took her chains off and Abraham Lincoln said, "You're free."

She said, "What does that mean?"

He said, "You're free to say whatever you want to say and free to go wherever you want to go."

Already recognizing his kindness she said, "I want to go with you."

That's ridiculous. You don't do that. That is grace. Grace creates the beauty we enjoy. Grace pursues us when we hide. Grace provides us with a salvation that is not free on God's part, but is free on your part. It is grace plus nothing.

Prayer: O God, thank you for that marvelous story of creation. Created in your image with a spiritual image and a spiritual power of choice and will, we chose to disobey. You did not kill us. You chose to search us out, pursued us and forgave us. Thank you for your marvelous grace. Help us to be found by that marvelous grace. In Jesus' name, Amen.

❧ Chapter Four ❧

Grace! It's Universal

TEXT: Genesis 12:1–5

CIT: Through grace God called Abraham to be blessed and to be a blessing.

THESIS: We are recipients of grace to be redistributors of grace.

PURPOSE: *Major objective:* ethical/actional

Specific objective: Through the power of the Holy Spirit, I hope to lead each of us in allowing God's grace to flow through us.

TITLE: "GRACE! IT'S UNIVERSAL"

INTRODUCTION

OUTLINE:

I.Grace upon the Individual—v. 2

II.Grace upon the Nation—v. 2

III.Grace upon the Universe—vv. 2–3

CONCLUSION

Scripture Reading: Genesis 12:1–5

The Lord had said to Abram, "Leave your country, your people, and your father's household and go to the land I will show you. I will make you into a great nation and I will bless you; I will make your name great, and you will be a blessing. I will bless those who bless you, and whoever curses you I will curse; and all peoples on earth will be blessed through you."

So Abram left, as the Lord had told him; and Lot went with him. Abram was seventy-five years old when he set out from Haran. He took his wife Sarai, his nephew Lot, all the possessions they had accumulated and the people they had acquired in Haran, and they set out for the land of Canaan, and they arrived there."

Introduction

Last Sunday's and this Sunday's texts and sermons I believe are foundational, pivotal for the understanding of much of what I am going to say the rest of the summer. We saw last week that grace began in the poetry of creation, that God created the universe as an act of grace. We fail sometimes to realize that if God had not created the universe, God would still be God. God Is. And God does not depend upon the universe for affirmation in God's being. God Is. Out of God's Isness and through grace, God created a beautiful universe such as we enjoy.

Seated on the deck last night after that brief storm and watching the magnificent sunset, I was awed by the realization that as I enjoyed that moment, there were literally millions of other individuals who were and would be enjoying the sunset that evening. I saw it as an act of grace, a moment of grace.

Grace in its beginning creates, and grace pursues us when we hide as Adam and Eve did. God's graceful voice calls out, "Where are you? Let me find you. Come out of your hiding," in order for God to provide for us forgiveness, removal of the shame, removal of the guilt. So grace in its beginning creates the beauty of which we enjoy, pursues us when we hide because of our sins, and provides forgiveness for us in the clothing God provided there in the garden.

I. Grace upon the Individual

Our text this morning is again out of the text of Genesis 12:1–5. I remember so very, very clearly the first time I ever read that passage of Scripture. I was not graced to have two parents in my childhood as many of you, nor was I graced to come up in a church-attending home, although I would say it was a home of faith. I did not attend church as a child. I came to faith as a twenty-one year old. Totally ignorant of the Scriptures, touched in a moment of sickness with the mumps by God's grace, I made a commitment of my life to a God I knew so very little about. I started trying to read the Scriptures to understand who this God was that I had made a commitment to. At that time, I was an eighth-grade dropout in the food business, married with two children and another one on the way. I started reading the Scriptures and I couldn't pronounce half of the words. I got over to so-in-so begat so-in-so and I couldn't pronounce the long name and I didn't quite know what begot meant in that context and went from book to book trying to understand. I got over to "Palms" (Psalms) and that didn't make a whole lot of sense. Then I read the book of "Job" (pronounced as synonym for work) and it didn't help me a whole lot. I got over to St. Matthew and it was a little more helpful.

Finally, I settled into the Book of John and that is very, very clear and simple. There in the book of John is where I met the Lord and made a faith commitment. I believe, not having been brought up in the church, that when I came to faith and came to the church, I came with a different perspective. I will not say I came with an objectivity, because objectivity is an illusion. We live under the illusion that this person is objective or that person is objective or maybe I'm objective about something, but objectivity is an illusion and it is relative. So I may come with a little less or maybe a little more objectivity than some do. But I do know I come with a sense of irreverence at some part and am sacrilegious as my critics would say at another part. But I come with a mind that questions. When I came to this text, I was startled by it. I was startled in that God picked a person out of the blue, it seemed, and said to Abram, I want to bless you. I want to make your name great. I want to grow a nation for you. I'll bless those who bless you and curse those who curse you. I remember looking at that and saying, "Why? Why? Why, God, would you just pick someone out of the blue?"

Of course, John Calvin would say God is sovereign. Whatever God wants to do, that's it. End of question. Just drop it and go on. But I have never been a good Presbyterian and I was never a good Baptist, so I don't just go on. I question and I wonder. I had never read Acts 10:34, nor had I ever read Matthew 20. I'd never read the part in Job that talks about God not being a respecter of persons. I had never read those, but there was deep within me a belief that God was not a respecter of persons. That was like being prejudiced toward this individual or that individual, so that deep question within me asked, "Why, God, would you choose this one person and your promise to bless him and do all those things for him? Why?" And I struggled and struggled with that. Of course in my later years, I learned about Acts 10:34, where it clearly says that God is no respecter of persons. And I can't impress upon you what an awesome revelation that was to Peter. Go back and read that tenth chapter of Acts and you will find Peter up on this housetop awaiting dinner and here is the absolute best definition of hypnosis you'll ever read anywhere. Peter says, "While in a trance, I saw a vision." And here's what Peter saw. He saw it not once, not twice, but three times to confirm it. Peter saw this sheet, a bedsheet of some type, lowered out of Heaven down to where he was on that rooftop. On the sheet were all kinds of animals to eat. I guess some of the animals Peter normally ate, but then there were those a good Jew would never touch—pigs, snakes, and the like. Go to the eleventh chapter of Leviticus and you will read all that good stuff that good Jews will not eat. If it splits the hoof completely and it chews the cud, those two things, then they will eat it. If not, they don't eat it. "It is detestable," the eleventh chapter of Leviticus says, "it is unclean." And Peter sees this sheet lowered with all this non-edible stuff in it, and a voice comes out of Heaven and says to Peter, "Kill and eat."

And Peter says, "No. No way will I eat that stuff. That stuff is unclean."

Second time, same vision, same voice.

Third time, same vision, same voice. Peter comes out of the trance. Immediately there's a knock on the door. He goes down. There's a Gentile down there that says, "Peter, there's a group of us over at the house who would like for you to come talk to us about Jesus Christ and God."

And Peter says, in one of those gestalt moments, "Aha. I see Lord what you are trying to say. That there's nothing unclean. You are the Creator and the Maker of us all." And Peter then goes to the Gentile house and preaches. They receive the Holy Spirit, salvation, and I say to you, had that not happened, the church as we know it today would not exist. The church as we know it today would not exist had that event not taken place, because Christianity started out with the Jews. It was a closed community. It was of the Jews. The Jews had nothing to do with the Gentiles. They would not eat in their homes, would not fellowship with them. They were a closed subject. I want you to see how God did it. God did it with hypnosis. God, the Great Hypnotist. Peter in a trance sees a vision. Then he puts the two together and says, "Aha! God is also of the Gentiles." And in that beautiful tenth chapter there is the verse where Peter says, "I now understand. God is no respecter of persons." Aha!

II. Grace upon the Nation

Notice the grace upon Abraham. Abraham was graced. He is to be the recipient of untold blessings, and the people who come from his seed are to be a nation. And this nation Israel is to be the recipient of untold blessings. But the answer was right there in the text. I just got so caught up in my bias, so caught up in my prejudice, so blinded by my own background I could not see it. For, you see, it says in our text twice, "I'll bless you." The word "bless" is there five times. "I'll bless you." Why?—"in order for you to be a blessing." Abraham, I want to make your name great. I want to make your descendents as numerous as the sands on the seashore, as numerous as the stars in the sky. I want to bless you in order for you to be a blessing." Wow! There's your answer.

God blessed an individual and said, "Out of your loins I'll build a nation to bless," and the purpose behind all of this is universal blessing.

And are we not aware that the three great monotheistic faiths of the world go back to this text right here? The beginning of Judaism—right here. The beginning of Christianity—right here. (Abraham is listed seventy to eighty times in the New Testament.) The beginning of Islam is right here. And it is these three great faiths that cling to the one and only God. God Is God. Call God Allah. Call God Yahweh. Call God Jesus. All three of these great monotheistic faiths go back to this text right here as their beginning point.

Let me read you a passage out of the Koran in relationship to this. It is called the Creed of Abraham:

> And they say be Jews or Christians, you shall be guided, say thou nay rather, the Creed of Abraham, a man of pure faith. He was no idolater. We believe in God and in that which has been sent down to us and sent down on Abraham, Ishmael, Isaac, Jacob, and the Tribes and that which was given to Moses and Jesus and the Prophets and their Lord, we make no division between any of them and to Him, God, we surrender.[6]

Did you hear that? In Karen Armstrong's book, *The Battle for God,* she quotes Mulla Sadra, who is a mystical philosopher. I was just amazed when I read, "We must return to the pure original vision of Abraham."[7] Wow! What is he saying? We must return to the belief that we are blessed, graced, for one reason and for one reason only—that we might be grace. We're blessed that we might be a blessing. We're graced that we might become grace. God is no respecter of persons. I don't think we can hear that. Although I have tried to describe it, I don't think we can hear how awesomely impacting Peter's vision was.

For example, suppose the Camden Bulldogs have a football jamboree tonight and no one but the Baptists are allowed. The only ones who can be there are Baptists. So the stadium in Camden is filled with Baptists. They are all Baptist. And before the game starts, out of the darkness of the night there is a huge celestial bar lowered right down in the middle of the field. It is filled with every liquor you could possibly think of. It is loaded. And this booming voice comes from Heaven and says, "Drink up." Can you imagine that? Baptists say, "No, we don't do that.

That's unclean." Can you imagine it? Maybe that will help us a little to understand what Peter was faced with, and the awesome realization that came to him that God's grace is not just for the Jews; that God's grace is for all of us. God's ridiculous affirmation of us is universal. Absolutely universal. We can't hear that even yet.

III. Grace upon the Universe

I was working as a therapist with a person who was in a deep state of ungrace. It was a hard session. I had earned my money. He wrote out his check to me and handed it to me at the close of the session. I tore it in half and then into four pieces and handed it back to him.

He said, "I don't understand."

I said, "I worked hard for that. I deserve that. You have just been graced."

"I don't know what that means."

I said, "Well, you think about it and next week we'll start the session on this act of grace."

During the week he calls and says, "I'm troubled by that. Grace is a theological term. I don't need a preacher. I don't need a pastor. I don't need a daddy. I don't need a Sunday School teacher. I'm not coming back next week and talk about grace. If I have to, we'll just terminate."

And I said, "OK. Maybe we need to terminate." I regretted that I'd leave him in a state of ungrace, but until that becomes a realization to him, no matter what I do as a therapist, he's stuck. I'm wasting my time, wasting his money—tear the check up, give it back and let him go.

Grace. God's ridiculous affirmation of humankind. Wow.

I want to read you something that Nancy Ore, a female seminary student wrote. The first time I read it, I read it as a father and I cried. The second time I read it, I read it as a husband and I cried. The third time I read it, I read it as a pastor and I cried. The fourth time I read it,

I read it as a counselor and I cried. I'll try not to cry this morning. God help us to hear it wherever we are:

It's not enough, said her father, that you get all A's each quarter, play Mozart for your kinfolk, win starred first in concerts, you must come home on your wedding night.

It's not enough, said her mother, that you smile at Aunt Lockwood, take cookies to the neighbors, keep quiet while I'm napping, you must cure my asthma.

It's not enough, said her husband, that you write letters to my parents, fix pumpkin pie and pastry, forget your name is Bauer, you must always, you must never.

It's not enough, said her children, that you make us female brownies, tend our friends and puppies, buy us Nike tennis, you must let us kill you.

It's not enough, said her pastor, that you teach the second graders, change the cloths and candles, kneel prostrate at the alter, as long as there are starving children in the world you must not eat without guilt.

It's not enough, said her counselor, that you struggle with the demons, integrate your childhood, leave when time is over, you must stop crying, clarify your poetic symbols, and not feel that you are not enough.

I give up, she said, I'm not enough and lay down into the deep, pocket of night to wait for death. She waited and finally her heart exploded. Her breathing stopped.

They came with stretcher, took off her clothes, covered her with linen, then went away and left her locked in the deep blue pocket tomb.

The voice said, "You Are Enough. Naked, crying, bleeding, nameless, starving, sinful, 'You Are Enough.' Then the third day she sat up, asked for milk and crackers, took a ritual bath with angels, dressed herself with wings, and flew away.[8]

Conclusion

Grace is realizing You Are Enough. You are so much and God loves you so deeply that God became one of us, lived among us to grace us, died on our behalf saying to us, "You are enough." And when we realize that we have been graced, and out of that grace we are enough, there will be a deep longing within us to be grace to others. I ask you, what would it be like if our Jewish world, our Christian world, our Islamic world, if all of the Jews, all of the Christians, and all of the Muslims went back to this text and said we have been graced to be grace? What would our world be like? Instant fighting would stop in Israel. Instantly, bickering throughout our world, squabbles between our denominations would end. When we realize we are graced, and that grace says, "You are enough, share it; you have been graced to be redistributors of grace," I ask you, imagine what our world would be like.

Prayer: O God, maybe the poet was inspired, maybe the philosopher heard the words from you when he said we must return to the pure, original vision of Abraham. The vision that says I want to bless you in order for you to bless others. I want you to be my channel through which I bless others. Bless, grace to be grace. Jesus help us to see that vision. In Jesus' name. Amen.

❦ Chapter Five ❧

Grace! It's Amazing

TEXT: 2 Kings 4:1–7

CIT: A widow was in debt facing the loss of her sons, and Elisha's act of grace saved her family.

THESIS: Grace may come to us through the use of what we have.

PURPOSE: *Major objective:* supportive

Specific objective: Through the power of the Holy Spirit, I hope to lead each of us in making available to God all that we are and all that we have.

TITLE: "GRACE! IT'S AMAZING"

INTRODUCTION

OUTLINE:

I. Amazing Grace Comes Through Shared Awareness—v. 1

II. Amazing Grace Comes Through Utilizing What You Have—v. 2

III. Amazing Grace Comes Through Personal Faith—vv. 3–6

CONCLUSION

Scripture Reading: 2 Kings 4:1–7

The wife of a man from the company of the prophets cried out to Elisha, "Your servant my husband is dead, and you know that he revered the Lord. But now his creditor is coming to take my two boys as slaves."

Elisha replied to her, "How can I help you? Tell me, what do you have in your house?"

"Your servant has nothing there at all," she said, "except a little oil."

Elisha said, "Go around and ask all your neighbors for empty jars. Don't ask for just a few. Then go inside and shut the door behind you and your sons. Pour oil into all the jars, and as each is filled, put it to one side."

She left him and afterward shut the door behind her and her sons. They brought the jars to her and she kept pouring. When all the jars were full, she said to her son, "Bring me another one."

But he replied, "There is not a jar left." The oil stopped flowing.

She went and told the man of God, and he said, "Go, sell the oil and pay your debts. You and your sons can live on what is left."

Introduction

Is that not an amazing story? Is that not a fascinating story? The fascinating, amazing story of grace. Grace almost always is a surprise, unprepared for, unexpected, undeserved, unmerited. Grace is an "Ah ha!" experience.

Let's look at this story a little closer and I believe in the midst of its amazingness, in the midst of its spontaneity and surprise, I believe we can find some principles that will help prepare the soil of our own lives. Not that such preparation can dictate the surprise. Our faith cannot capture grace, but I think we can prepare ourselves in such a way that we are more potentially recipients of that "Ah ha," surprise, spontaneous, unmerited dowsing of God's grace.

I. Amazing Grace Comes Through Shared Awareness

Amazing grace comes first of all I believe through awareness. I want you to notice her awareness. I want you to contrast awareness with denial. She is a minister's wife, a prophet's wife, and her minister husband, prophet husband, dies. She is extremely poor. The company of the prophets, as it's referred to in the Bible, did its job well. The church usually does its job well. You know the church's responsibility is to keep the minister poor, and God's responsibility is to keep him humble.

This past December when I bought a new truck, one of my Elders looked at it and said, "Ah, a new truck."

And I detected something there, maybe my own projection. And I said, "Yes, y'all are not doing your job well."

And he said, "What do you mean?"

And I said, "Well, the church's job is to keep me poor and God's job is to keep me humble."

He said, "Huh. Neither one of us is doing our job, are we?"

But here is this minister's wife whose husband has died and she is left destitute. The debtors are claiming her sons. The creditors are claiming her sons for payment. Now she can live in denial. "I know the man. He would do that. He's just spouting off. He's trying to push me into paying the debt. I just don't have the money to pay. He's not going to do that." She may well live in denial right up until the creditor knocks on the door and says, "Where are the lads?"

You know we have people who do that. They are just locked into denial of their situation. A married couple comes to my office. He's there because his wife brought him and I look at him and say, "Do you have a problem with alcohol?"

He says, "No."

And I say, "Have you ever had a DUI?"

And he says, "Yeah."

And I say, "How many?"

"About three."

"You have a problem with alcohol?"

"No."

I mean this man is just locked up in that cage of denial.

My mother-in-law has breast cancer and is facing surgery next week. It was discovered through the first mammogram she ever had in her life. She's seventy years old. Her first mammogram discovers the cancer and she says to us, "Every time I go to the doctor, they find something wrong. I'm not going anymore. I was doing fine until I went." She is just locked up in that denial. Just bury your head in the sand. It's going to go away. It's not going to happen.

I want you to notice in the Scripture the minister's wife's awareness. She is aware that there is a problem. This creditor has said, "You owe this money, you're not able to pay it, and I'm coming for your sons as slaves for that money." She becomes aware of this and says, "I have to do something about this." But I want you to notice the second step. Grace, amazing grace, can come into our lives when we are aware of our need of grace. And then when we are willing to share that awareness. Do you notice what she did? Do you see that clearly? Did she lock herself up in her house and pray, "Lord, do something about this situation. Lord, you've got to do something about this situation. This man is coming to take my two sons. You have got to do something about this situation."

You know we are hearing a lot about flooding these days, out in Houston and in Louisiana. You've probably heard that flood story. This guy is a faithful person and this flood comes through his town, probably in Houston, and he's up on the eave of his porch praying to God to deliver him from this flood. This boat comes by and someone says, "You need some help?" And he waves them on. "I'm praying God's going to take care of me." So the water keeps rising and he moves on up to the very eave on top of the house and a second boat comes by. "Hey, you need some help?" He waves them on. "God's going to take care of me. I'm waiting. I'm faithful." A little while later, a helicopter comes by and someone calls to him and says, "You need some help?" The man said, "No, God's going to take care of me." Well, the water comes up over the house and pushes the house down into the river and he drowns. There he is in Heaven and he says to God in a very accusatory term, "I'm a believer. I had faith that You were going to deliver me. I'm faithful." God said, "Yeah, you are a faithful idiot. I sent two boats and a helicopter by and you wouldn't take either one of them."

So grace often comes to us through someone else, through someone else's hands. When we are willing to share the need of that grace, do you hear what she does? She becomes aware of the need of grace in her life and she cries out, "Elisha, do you remember my husband? Godly man, loved the Lord, was one of your band. He's dead. The creditors are coming after my sons as payment. You've got to do something." Not only does she become aware of her situation in need of grace, she shares that need with someone else. When we're able to make that first step, many of us get caught in that second step because we won't share it.

A number of years ago there was a very critical turning point, the benchmark experience in my own personal therapy. One day with my therapist, I was trying to fill the time with something to say—you know we do that sometimes. We try to talk about something that's not necessarily related to why we are there. So I was just trying to fill up time. And I told him about this story about when I was a child in Tennessee. They would ship me up there often to my great uncle in Rogersville, Tennessee. The first time I went I was about eight or nine, and Uncle George and I were looking for a calf one Sunday afternoon. We were walking by the shores of Cherokee River, which is now Cherokee Lake. They put dams on the end of it and it became a lake. About 500–600 yards on the other side of the lake, he hears a little calf bellowing. He says, "That's my calf." So we get in this homemade canoe and paddle on the other side of the lake, and that's not his calf. So we're paddling back and we're about halfway in the middle of the 400–500 yard wide lake. It's early in the spring right after school's out, and he says to me, "Curley," that's what he always called me, "can you swim?"

I said, "Yes sir."

He said, "Shuck your clothes and hit it."

Well, I thought that was a good idea, so I dropped my pants and dove off the end of the canoe, and of course as I did, I pushed the canoe away from me. I came up out of the water and turned around and this old man was in the canoe paddling just as hard as he could. So I started swimming to catch up with the canoe. He kept paddling and he started laughing. He was just giggling and laughing and paddling that canoe. The canoe kept getting farther and farther away. I'm paddling just as hard as I can paddle and I'm losing ground. I remember thinking as I'm just stoking it as hard as I can and as fast as I can to get to Uncle George, "This old fool's going to let me die." Well, I guess he gets tired and he quits. I catch up with the canoe, get in it, and we go on home.

I share that little tidbit with my therapist. Well, my therapist loved to do those weekend kind of deals where you go in on Friday afternoon and you do therapy with a group of people Friday night, all day Saturday, and then they bundle you up in this white blanket and send you home on the end of Saturday. We're having one of these retreats at his retreat-house and he says, "Gene, get on the floor on your back."

I trust my therapist so I got on the floor on my back. He put two people on the right and two people on the left, and he had two people on each arm. He weighs over 300 lbs. and he sat on my midsection and put his big arm across my chest and looked at me in the face and said, "Get up."

That deep crazy part of me believed that I could actually get up. Then for about 30 minutes I fought with every ounce of my strength and every fiber of my being and then it moved into that almost psychotic realm where I was screaming and yelling and thrashing, trying to get those people off of me. I finally began to slow down a little bit with everything exhausted. Again, he got close to my face and said, "How are you going to get up?"

And I said, "Will y'all please let me up?"

Every one of them just jumped up. Then we huddled around and started processing that, and he asked me to share that little story again. Then he said to me, "You would have allowed your Uncle George to keep paddling until you drowned without saying, 'Stop! I'm in trouble.'" And the truth is I would have.

There are many of us just like that. We will deny ourselves grace. We'll not receive the abundance of God's mercy and God's presence and God's giftedness simply because we're not aware of the need of it, nor will we share it with anyone. When we will not share that need, no one knows and no one can be the instrument, the hands of God's grace in our lives. We get locked up in pride, locked up in grandiosity, locked up in denial, and we will not share out of our awareness with someone else who cares what we want, what we need, what we must have.

II. Amazing Grace Comes Through Utilizing What You Have

Notice the woman. Amazing grace came to her because she was aware of her situation and she shared her situation. Now I want you to notice the second principle. Elisha says to her, "What do you have in the house?"

She says, "Nothing." Did you notice that? She says nothing. Nothing at all. Do you hear what Elisha's asking her? "You are in need of help, you're in need of grace, you're in need of a miracle. What do you have in your house?"

"Nothing. Not a thing."

Why did Elisha ask her that? Could he not just pick up a bucket of sand and said I'll turn this into gold? God will turn this into gold? Sure he could have. God could do whatever God wants to do. But Elisha said to her what do you have, wanting her to be a participant and not become dependent. That's the greatest sin of our welfare program for all these decades. We've not asked anyone, what do you have?' What are you capable of putting in? What are you capable of giving? I want to help you to become a participant in your grace, in your miracle. We just say, here it is. Go use it. God said through Elisha, what do you have? And then it's like she has this second thought. She says, "Nothing except a little oil."

I am reminded of the story in the fourth chapter in Exodus. God is dealing with Moses through this burning bush and God wants Moses to go down to Egypt and deliver God's people. Moses starts this litany of pitiful excuses. Right in the middle of that God says to Moses, "Moses, what do you have in your hand?"

And Moses says, "A stick."

A stick? A shepherd's crook. It's just a stick. An inanimate piece of wood. And God says to Moses, "Throw it on the ground."

"Throw it on the ground?"

"Yes. Throw it on the ground."

"Why?" Moses doesn't really say that. I say that. I'd be saying that.

God said, "Throw it on the ground." And Moses threw it on the ground. It became a snake. God said, "Pick it up." That's worse than throwing it down. Well, Moses picks it up and it turns back into the stick. "Moses what do you have in your hand?"

Moses really needed help. He started that litany of excuses again and God said to Moses, "Put your stick down, let's just talk about you. What's that right there?"

Moses said, "That's my hand."

God said, "Put it in your cloak." That's where Napoleon got the idea.

So Moses puts his hand in his cloak, then pulls it back out and it has leprosy, a dreaded disease of that time. God said, "Put it back in there."

"I ain't putting it back in there. It'll touch the rest of my body and I'll have a leprous chest."

"No, put it back in there."

So he puts it back in there and pulls it out and it's clean.

God says, "Moses, what do you have in your hand?"

I was also reminded of that beautiful David story in the seventeenth chapter of first Samuel. David, a young shepherd boy, goes over to where his brothers are encamped to bring them some food. When he gets there he finds that they are camped on one side of the creek and the Philistines are camped on the other side of the creek, and three times a day a nine-foot giant called Goliath comes out on the bank of the creek and denounces them, calls them bad names. David says, "Why doesn't someone go take care of him?"

And they said, "Well, why don't you go take care of him?'

He said, "Alright, I will." So David starts down there and King Saul sees David and says, "Now wait a minute, son. What are you going to do?"

He says, "I'm going down there and take care of Goliath."

"You're unprepared. You don't have anything." Saul is seven feet tall. Saul says, "Here's my tunic. Put on my armor. Here's my sword, here's my helmet." Can't you just see that kid? You know it's just like children playing dress up. Here he is with a helmet on his head. He can't even see out from under it. The sword is dragging, making a track in the sand, and the armor is hanging down to his ankles. David gets all this on and says, "I can't do this. I can't handle this." So he takes all this stuff off and says, "Give me my sling shot. That's all I want. Just give me my sling." He takes his sling picks up five smooth round rocks and puts one in that sling and hits Goliath between the eyes and he falls dead.

"What do you have?"

"Nothing. I don't have anything."

"Yeah you do. What do you have?"

"Well, I have a little oil."

We miss the grace of God often by simply not being aware of what it is we have.

"What can you do?"

"Nothing. I can't teach. I can't pray in public. I can't do this or that. I have nothing in my hand. I have no talent in my body. I have no gift in my being. I have nothing."

And all the while, you're missing this awesome, amazing grace response of God while God is saying to you, "What do you have in your hand?"

"What do you have? What do you have that I can use and make miraculous?

"I've got a little oil."

III. Amazing Grace Comes Through Personal Faith

OK. Here's the third point. Amazing grace comes to us through the exercise of our personal faith. Everything could have broken down right here. Elisha says to her, "You got a little oil in the house?"

"Yes."

"Do you have any empty jars?"

"Not at home."

"Well, you and your boys go out throughout the community and collect all the empty jars that you can collect."

Can't you just hear it? "That's stupid. Why do I want empty jars? I've got enough trash and litter at my house already, and then I've got to go out into the community and ask for empty jars? I can see going over there asking for a cup of sugar. But to go out there and ask for an empty jar, they're going to ask what am I going to do with it. I don't know what to tell them. I don't know what to say." A faith response always carries a little bit of humility. Trust is involved. There's no trust without humility. Faith is involved. There's no trust and faith without humility.

Elisha says, "Go into the community. Find some jars. Take them back to the house. Close the doors. Start filling them up with oil."

She could have had a thousand excuses. But she's faithful. Faith always has an element of action or it's not faith. That's why James in his little Epistle says, "Faith without the action of works is dead."

Conclusion

Last year Linda and I went to Costa Rica on vacation. We had read in these little brochures about going to the rain forest and doing a little canopy trip there. The brochure looked wonderful. Here was a person, and it's always a beautiful blue-eyed blonde, strapped in her gear and she's holding on to a cable. She sees monkeys hanging from the trees behind her and parrots and peacocks. She's just gliding along down through the rain forest on this cable. It really did look good. So we signed up for the canopy trip and we walked a ways down through the rain forest to finally get to a huge tree at the edge of the forest. There's a wooden ladder going up this tree. We have two wonderful guides with us that are doing a beautiful job. One goes up the ladder and tells us to climb up too. So we all climb this homemade 30–40 foot ladder. It is similar to a deer stand, only a little bit larger, but not much. We had been instructed on how to wear our harness. A guide gave us a helmet and tells us a helmet won't do any good if we fall. Why wear the thing? It just makes you feel better. So we're up on this platform and this steel cable is running from this tree and just disappears into the forest. We were given more instructions and the guide said he was going to hook up first, go on over, and wait for us. We still had in our minds this leisurely meandering through the rain forest. Well, he gets hooked up to this thing, steps off the platform, and gets going, "sssssssshew." He couldn't have seen a monkey if there had been a hundred of them hanging in a tree. He just disappeared into the woods. We saw him vaguely through the trees as he reached the next platform. The other guide turns around and asks who's going. Linda says, "I'm going first."

I thought, "Wow, my wife."

When we all finally make it over to the other side, I say to her, "That was a real brave thing to do."

41

She said, "Brave, nothing. If I had waited, I'd have climbed back down that ladder."

Faith is hooking up and going. Not knowing exactly what's out there. Trusting the instructions. Trusting the cable. Trusting God, needing grace here, okay? Get on it and "ssssssshew."

Faith is always taking a step, doing an action. Everything here would have broken down if this woman had said, "That's embarrassing to go into the community and do that. I am not doing that." But amazing grace came into her life because she was aware of the need of it. She shared that need with Elisha. She used what she had, a little bit of oil, and she took personal responsibility for the action of her faith. When we do that, those spontaneous, undeserved, unmerited acts of grace can be available to us.

Prayer: Oh Lord, thank you for this amazing story. We truly do understand it as amazing. But Lord as we look at it, it is also amazing that we are so ungraced and graceless. Help us to see these elements that prepared her as a fertile field for the sowing of your grace. Help us in our own lives to prepare to do so. May it be so. In Jesus' name. Amen.

Naaman's servants went to him and said, "My father, if the prophet had told you to do some great thing, would you not have done it? How much more, then, when he tells you, 'Wash and be cleansed!' " So he went down and dipped himself in the Jordan seven times, as the man of God had told him, and his flesh was restored and became clean like that of a young boy.

Then Naaman and all his attendants went back to the man of God. He stood before him and said, "Now I know that there is no God in all the world except in Israel. Please accept now a gift from your servant."

The prophet answered, "As surely as the Lord lives, whom I serve, I will not accept a thing." And even though Naaman urged him, he refused.

Introduction

The title of this message, "Grace! It's Ridiculous," has been the second object of considerable criticism of this whole series—the first being the title, *Grace Is Not a Blue-eyed Blonde.* And to that charge I freely admit the title is sacrilegious. "Grace! It's Ridiculous," I also freely admit, is also sacrilegious. But I say to you as I said to you once before, grace itself is sacrilegious.

The French philosopher in his book *The Fall* talks about a spitting cell where they would put a prisoner to shame and humiliate the prisoner. The cell was so small that the prisoner could only stand, and so tight that he could not move his arms nor turn his head. In front of his face was an opening. Every time a guard walked by that cell, the guard would spit in the face of the inmate. All the inmate could do was close his eyes.[9] Grace spits in the face of religion and the name of that spit is Jesus Christ. Grace is the most unique theological expression the theological world has ever known, and at our core we are deeply, deeply fearful of grace. We're fearful about what grace does and what it says. It is dangerous to talk about really the essence of grace. One man did and they nailed him to a tree. Grace is shocking. It IS ridiculous.

I've looked the word up. I know what it means. Webster's first definition of the word is laughable. I want you to see the laugh-ability of grace in this text. Here's a soldier in a foreign army, Aaron's army. Apparently a very brave and valiant soldier, who in fact is accredited for establishing the kingdom of Aaron. Did you notice the "but"? A valiant soldier, brave soldier, highly praised and esteemed . . . but. He has leprosy. He has a horrible social disease. Were it not for his standing, he would be an outcast to the community and would be begging at some city gate for his well-being. He is an unacceptable. He has leprosy. That strikes at part of the problem of grace.

Let me explain. You're at a pig-picking on the lake. You're at some party talking about the Lakers basketball team or the speedway in Darlington. You might be sharing a new fudge recipe or talking about flowers or whatever. You want to bring an end to that conversation? You want to introduce a spirit of disquiet? Just start talking about grace. They won't say ugly things to you. They'll just look at you with that deer in the headlights look. They won't respond because they don't know what to say. Just start talking about grace and watch the people. Oh, Myrtle, Sam. They'll just start walking away. It is uncomfortable. And part of why it is uncomfortable is we are all in need of it! We don't like to admit it. We're all lepers. We're all sinful. We're all reprobates. We don't like to be reminded of it. We don't like to be reminded of our sin. We don't like to be reminded of our ugliness. We don't like to be reminded of our failures and our mistakes. And grace lifts us. You have to be in need of it to talk about it. We don't like to be in need of it. Grace is undeserved and unmerited. It's a surprise. You can't earn it. It also speaks about the inability, the human inability, to please God. So we like to talk about things at the church, in our community, in our organization, and what we do, and all of that good stuff that enhances our humanity and speaks well of who we are and what we do. Don't start talking about reprobates in need of grace, grace doing something for us that we cannot do ourselves. We don't like that. So the next time you want to end a conversation at one of your parties, you want to go speak to someone else, just mention grace. Watch it shut down.

I. Grace Seems Ridiculous When It Confronts Our Pride

Grace is ridiculous. It's laughable. I hope you see that in the text. Here's a man in all of his greatness who has leprosy. Either he or one of his sergeants has gone out and captured folks. They've captured a little

Israelite girl. She is aware of the prophet in Israel. She says to Naaman's wife, "Ah, if the master were in Israel, he could be cured of his leprosy." Now apparently she thought something of her master and mistress, but don't get the idea of the happy slave. We tried to promote that in the south years ago. It didn't work then and it won't work now. A slave is a slave. You won't find a happy slave. But she says to her mistress he ought to go. So Naaman approaches Aaron and shares the message with him. He takes all these gifts, sets of clothing, silver and gold, and piles all of this on. A letter goes to Israel [asking] to be cured. The king is upset, of course. He thinks King Aaron is setting him up, putting him in a Catch-22, and he's upset, but Elisha hears about it and says, "Send the fellow to me."

Now notice Naaman's expectation when he goes. He goes to the man of God's house and a messenger comes out. No Elisha but a messenger. The messenger comes out and says, "Here's what the prophet has said: 'Go to the Jordan River and dunk in it seven times and you will be cleansed of your leprosy.'"

Naaman goes away furious. Absolutely furious. You reckon he used the word ridiculous? "That's absolutely ridiculous. Look at the rivers in my own country." He names a couple. "I'm not going to that silly muddy river Jordan."

Any of you ever seen the Jordan? I never have, but I've read about it and heard about it. The impression I get is that it is a little like the Rio Grande.

I cut my teeth on Zane Grey's westerns. That's the only thing I ever started reading in my life that I wasn't made to read. I fell in love through reading Zane Grey's westerns. I had this burning desire to see the Rio Grande. Then I had an opportunity to see it as an adult. A friend of mine took me out there and we were on horseback and we came around this bend and he said, "Now prepare yourself," because he was a Zane Grey reader also. We had shared some stories that Zane Grey had written in and around Texas and Mexico. We came around this bend and, lo and behold, there it was. We rode the horses across it and it did not even cover their hooves.

I said, "In South Carolina we do not call this a river. We call it a creek." And I can just imagine someone saying to me, "Dunk in the Rio Grande."

"No, I'll just go back to the Catawba River. No, I'll not get in that mud hole."

Naaman was insulted. At least the man of God could have come out and called upon his God and put his hands over my plague. God would have come down to me. Do you sense his pride? "Ah, God could have spoken through this mighty prophet and I would have been healed. Go dunk in that river? I don't think so."

He went away in a rage. In a rage grace smacks us in our pride. "I don't need that. I'll just join the church. I'll give 'em my money. I'll be baptized. I'll join some committees. I'll be in the Presbyterian Women if they will let me." You know, we'll do all these wonderful things and get involved in all this stuff. "Dunk in the river?" I don't think so. I don't think so. It's ridiculous. It's laughable. It's foolish. I'll not do that.

II. Grace Seems Ridiculous When It Calls for Humility

One of his servants goes to Naaman and says, "Sir, if they had told you to do this mighty and great thing, 'Go conquer this neighboring nation and you'll be healed,' what would you have done? You would have done it. All he asked you to do was to dip in the water seven times." Isn't that just like us? I believe with every fiber of my being that if today what it took to be a Christian was to memorize verbatim Mathew, Mark, Luke, and John, there would be more Christians then than there would be now. You'd see it on your automobile tags: Christian, John Doe. Look what I did. You'd see it on your mailboxes: Christian, John Doe. You'd have it on your business cards: Christian, John Doe. It's something I could do. But grace says it's not something you can do. It is unmerited, undeserved. It is a gift that God wants to lavish on us. Jesus came with that message and Jesus' world said, "No, no, no. You've got to keep the law." And he wouldn't keep the law as they understood it and he wouldn't talk about it if they talked about it. And they nailed him to a tree.

Grace is ridiculous because it smacks us in our sinfulness, it smacks us in our inability to save ourselves, it smacks us in our pride, and we reject it and turn away. The church, although it is the most unique and marvelous gift of the church, is afraid of it. We're afraid to say to our people, "It is through grace plus nothing that you are saved. No obligations. It is free, underserved." It is dunking in the Jordan. We don't preach that because we are afraid to. We're fearful that our people would not come back. They won't feel obligated. They won't join our committees. They are free of their guilt. We want them obligated. We don't want them free of their guilt. Hey, I might not have enough in the treasury to pay my salary. So it's grace. But if you've really been graced, you'll join our committees. You'll join our churches. You'll be baptized. You'll give us your money if you've really been recipients of grace. And grace says it is grace plus nothing. That's fearful. That's ridiculous. It is the greatest message the church has but we're fearful of sharing it. We will not trust grace.

III. Grace Seems Ridiculous When It Cannot Be Purchased

Naaman goes down to the river, dunks himself seven times, and his skin is like the skin of a child. He comes back to Elisha's house with praise and adoration for Elisha's God and he says, "Take all these wonderful gifts." Do you hear what he's trying to do now? Grace has obligated him to grace. And he wants to purchase it. "Let me pay you so I won't feel obligated to grace. Let me pay you so I won't feel grace in order to grace." If I am a recipient of grace, it says to me at the core of my being, BE GRACEFUL. No, I don't like that. I want to buy it; take the money; take the gold; take the silver; let me free of this grace obligation. Elisha says, "No, you keep your money." Grace cannot be bought. It is not for sale. It is not offered on the bartering block of our economics. Grace, the most radical understanding of the theological world, is yet misunderstood.

Conclusion

Big Emma was a woman in Lubbock, Texas, who had a little shack by the railroad. Big Emma was a prostitute who sold and ran the numbers and bootleg liquor, and sold her body. She had a surprise which was a son. A hated surprise. An obligation she did not want. She named him Race Hoss Sample. She told him every day he was an inconvenience with her words and with the back of her hand and a foot in the stomach. Race Hoss took that kind of abuse until he was eleven years of age. At eleven he got on the rails that ran by his little shack and rode them away. Rode the rails with bums and hobos who beat him and abused him just like Big Emma had beat him and abused him until his body became large enough that he no longer had to take it and he could give it. Filled with his rage of rejection, sin, and unacceptance, he beat up anyone who got in his way. At eighteen the Army found him and drafted him into the Second World War. You can draft one but you cannot necessarily tame one. They could not tame Race Hoss. They couldn't even keep him in harness. Every other week or two he was AWOL. Raging on his peers and raging on his officers, he wound up with thirty-three years in the Texas State Penitentiary. You may lock a man up, but you may not tame him. The prison system in Texas believed they could. Their way to tame him was to put him in the Tomb, which was a 4' x 8' concrete building in the basement with a small opening in the concrete slab door just large enough to get a tin cup of water in. There they would place the inmate for 28 days, receiving a cup of water and a dry biscuit. On the sixth day they would receive a bowl of mush. At the back of this little 4' x 8' hole there was a slab of concrete missing, and that was the toilet. The stench of everyone who had been there before filled that place. For sixteen years Race Hoss, every time he would strike an officer, would be placed for twenty-eight days in the Tomb. In his sixteenth year he was placed once again in the Tomb for a 28-day stretch, but it was different, unusual, because when they threw him in, in his words, he went crazy. In the words of a psychotherapist, he had a psychotic break. But in the words of theology there is a different word. Let me read to you in his own words what he said about this experience:

"I ran around the walls. I rolled on the floor like a ball. I mauled myself scratching and tearing at my body. Slumped, exhausted on the slab, I covered my face with both hands and cried out, 'God help me, help me, help me.' A ray of light between my fingers slowly uncovered my face. The little cell was illuminated like a 40 watt light bulb turned on. The soft light soothed me and I no longer was afraid. Engulfed by a Presence, I felt it reassuring me. It comforted me. I breathed deeply and I never felt such well-being, so good, in all of my life. Safe. Love. The voice within talked through the pit of my belly: 'You're not an animal. You are a human being. Don't worry about a thing, but you must tell them about this experience.' After that God was real. God found me in the abyss of the burning hell, uplifted and fed my hungry soul and breathed new life into my nostrils."[10]

Race Hoss walked out of prison January 12, 1972, at 9:45 in the morning. The state of Texas gave him ten dollars. Hear what else the state of Texas gave him. He was the first ex-con to work out of the governor's office, the first one. He was the first ex-con ever to serve as a probation officer. The first ex-con ever to serve on the state bar of Texas as a division head. He was given the Liberty Bell award and named the Outstanding Crime Prevention Citizen of Texas in 1981. In 1976 he received a full pardon from the state of Texas and changed his name to Alfred Sample.[11] THAT, dear friends, is grace.

You can't control it. You can't pray for it enough to get it. It is a surprise and it is absolutely ridiculous.

Prayer: Oh Lord, we talk about being washed in the blood and there are those who laugh at us. There are those who say, "Someone died 2,000 years ago and that life is going to grace me today, I don't know about that. It sounds foolish." Lord help us. Help us to know you as a God who graces. A God who comes into our lives whether we've been prayed for or not. A grace who comes into our lives underserved, unmerited. Help us as your people to come to know it, live it and simply do what you told Race Hoss to do: "Share it." In Jesus' name. Amen.

∽ *Chapter Seven* ∾

Grace! It's Personified

TEXT:John 1:1–14

CIT: God's grace became human in the cosmic and historical person of Jesus Christ.

THESIS: God graced us through becoming one of us in the cosmic Christ.

PURPOSE: *Major objective:* doctrinal

Specific objective: Through the power of the Holy Spirit, I hope to lead each of us in affirming the grace of God through the cosmic Christ.

TITLE: "GRACE! IT'S PERSONIFIED"

INTRODUCTION

OUTLINE:

I. The Cosmic Christ Is the Logos of God—vv. 1, 14

II. The Cosmic Christ Is the Doxa of God—v. 14

III. The Cosmic Christ Is the Grace of God—v. 14

IV. The Cosmic Christ Is the Truth of God—v. 14

CONCLUSION

Dr. Eugene C. Rollins

Scripture Reading: John 1:1–14

In the beginning was the Word, and the Word was with God, and the Word was God. He was with God in the beginning.

Through him all things were made; without him nothing was made that has been made. In him was life, and that life was the light of men. The light shines in the darkness, but the darkness has not understood it.

There came a man who was sent from God; his name was John. He came as a witness to testify concerning that light, so that through him all men might believe. He himself was not the light; he came only as a witness to the light. The true light that gives light to every man was coming into the world.

He was in the world, and though the world was made through him, the world did not recognize him. He came to that which was his own, but his own did not receive him. Yet to all who received him, to those who believed in his name, he gave the right to become children of God—children born not of natural descent, human decision, or a husband's will, but born of God.

The Word became flesh and lived for a while among us. We have seen his glory, the glory of the one and only Son, who came from the Father, full of grace and truth.

(Note: This sermon was offered Sunday, July 1, 2001, two months before the terrorist attack on the World Trade Center Twin Towers, September 11, 2001.)

Prayer: Oh Lord, we praise you and thank you for this opportunity to gather in public worship. It is impossible to think about public worship without thinking about your grace, which makes it possible. It is almost impossible to think about America without thinking about your grace that has made it possible for all of the liberties and the freedoms that we enjoy and can call "graces and blessings"—grace, the unmerited, undeserved blessings of God. Oh God, if there is ever a country existing whose blessings are deeply unmerited and undeserved, it is this one. So we praise you and thank you not only for the privilege to gather publicly throughout our land and worship in freedom and in liberty, we give you praise and thanksgiving for all of the manifold blessings that we as a country enjoy. For all of those who have literally laid down their lives to make our freedom possible, we pause in this moment to praise you and thank you for them. For all of the dedicated servants who yet lay down their lives in service to maintain and keep our constitutional freedoms and liberty, we give you thanks and praise. As your blessings and graces abound, help us to have our praises and thanksgivings also to abound. In Jesus' name. Amen.

Introduction

For the past several weeks we have looked at grace in the Old Testament—it's beginning. Now we'll see grace personified. For the next few weeks we'll look at how this grace walked among us and lived among us. The Word of the Lord: "In the beginning was the Word and the Word was with God and the Word was God. He was with God in the beginning. Through him all things were made; without him nothing was made that has been made. In Him was life and that life was the life of men. The light shines in the darkness but the darkness has not understood it."

Let me pause there just for a second to say that this Greek word is almost impossible to be translated with one word, so I am going to use three. But the darkness has not understood, has not overcome, has not extinguished it, the light. There came a man who was sent from God. His name was John. He came as a witness to testify concerning that light so that through him all men might believe. He himself was not the light. He came only as a witness to the light. The true light that gives light to every man was coming into the world. He was in the world and though the world was made through him, the world did not recognize him. He came to that which was his own. But his own did not receive him. Yet to all who received him, to all those who believed in his name, he gave the right to become the children of God. Children born not of natural descent, human decision, or husband's will, but born of God. The Word became flesh and lived for a while among us. We have seen his glory, the glory of the one and only son who came from the Father full of grace and full of truth."

Look again at that 14th verse. I'd like for us to camp out there for 4 or 5 weeks, but we are unable to do so. Look at it again. The Word, the Logos, the Mind and Meaning of God became flesh. Lived for a while among us. We have seen His doxology, Glory, the glory of the one and only son who came from the Father full of Grace and full of truth.

I. The Cosmic Christ Is the Logos of God

Much is being debated and written today about distinguishing between the Jesus of history and the Christ of faith. Some call it the pre-Easter Jesus and the post-Easter Jesus. For those who divide Jesus up in these ways or try to think in these terms, they normally use Mark, Matthew, and Luke as the Gospels that talk about the historical Jesus, the Jesus of history, and the Gospel of John that talks about the post-Easter Jesus or the Christ of history, or the Christ I like to call the cosmic Christ. John's gospel was written about 100–105 A.D., meaning it was written about seventy years after Jesus lived, died, and resurrected. So by the time as it was forming and evolving, the church had given much thought to not only the historical Jesus but the cosmic Christ. Whereas, Luke took Jesus back to Adam and Matthew took Jesus back to Abraham, the cosmic Gospel of John takes Jesus back to the beginning. "In the beginning was the Word, the Logos, the mind and meaning of God." The mind and meaning of God existed before matter existed. And there in the mind and meaning of God this grace that became flesh existed. So it is a cosmic gospel. This was a beautiful hymn that was used in the church probably long before it was put into the form of the Gospel of John. We learn best as children through songs, hymns. How did you first learn about Jesus? Did you first learn about Jesus through the Scriptures? Probably not. Your first experience of Jesus was through Jesus loves me this I know for the Bible tells me so. So you learned that in song and that's the way the word of God was transmitted and evolved as the church was evolving. They learned about the Jesus of history and the cosmic Christ through song. This was one of those beautiful songs, one of those doxology poems, in the prelude in the gospel of John. It has so much wonderful truth for us that this cosmic Christ came as the Logos, the Word and the meaning of God. God's Word and God's

Meaning is involved in this act of grace of God becoming flesh and living among us.

II. The Cosmic Christ Is the Doxa of God

Then that next word, that we get our English word "doxology" from, the cosmic Christ became the glory of God. It's built upon that Old Testament word, *shekina,* that is illustrated when Moses came down off Mt. Sinai that the shekina glory of God surrounded him so that the people couldn't look at him. They had to cover their faces. So Jesus came as this shekina glory of God, this doxology of God. God sang this doxology and the song became flesh in Jesus the Christ. Jesus Christ the Word, the Mind and the Meaning of God, became the doxology of God and the grace of God.

You'll notice on the front of the bulletin, I define grace as God's Redemptive Acquittal Concerning Everyone. Now if there is anyone who wants to nail me for universalism, you've got your piece of evidence right there. God's redemptive grace came in Jesus Christ to acquit. That is a legal term. Senator Donald Holland is with us this morning. He has graced us by his presence this morning. Donald, we are glad to have you. You know, Don is a lawyer, and that is a legal term. To acquit means to set free from a sentence, a charge. Grace that came embodied in Jesus Christ was God's acquittal of us all. Read John 3:16, "For God so loved the world that he came," he came and became one of us, "that whosoever believeth in him shall not die, perish, but have everlasting life." We were existing under the charge of death, under the charge of sin, under the charge of guilt, under the charge of shame and God's doxology came in the form of Jesus the Christ to acquit, set free, throw off the charges, of all of us. In that beautiful verse, this doxology, this grace, is full of truth. You want to know the truth about what God believes about us? Do you want to know the truth? Look at Jesus Christ.

Years ago I was in a large church in Greenville, South Carolina. It was situated in one of those circumstances where a lot of people came and went visiting us. We averaged 20–35 visitors every service. One Sunday night I came out of the service and I could tell this man was lingering in the foyer. He had this huge Bible under his arms. It was large enough to be a lethal weapon. But out of respect I could tell it was weathered and worn. I had preached out of the Old Testament that night. He had that big old Bible and took it out from under his arm as he reached out to greet me with the other hand. As he let my hand go, he hit his Bible and he said, "Preach the red words." He looked me right in the eyes and said again, "Preach the red words." That night I had not preached the red words. If you don't know what the red words are, they are the words of Jesus in the Gospels. Well, I laughed him off as a little radical, a little fundamental. But the older I have become, the more brazen I have become. Maybe we ought to just throw out everything and throw off everything and just concentrate on the red words. If we really want to know the mind, the truth, and heart, and the meaning of what God wants to say to us, maybe we need to throw out everything the church has ever said about the Scriptures. Throw out everything the church has ever said about theology. Throw out what the rest of the book says about Jesus and just concentrate on the red words. Maybe the man was not so wrong.

Maybe he was not so wrong to shake his Bible in a preacher's face and say, "If you want to do your job best, preach the red words." For you see what I have experienced in my life and my relationship with people is that God has awesomely graced us in Jesus Christ—this awesome redemptive acquittal of us all where God says to us, you do not have to live under shame, you do not have to live under guilt. I have come and walked among you and lived an example to set you free. But we strive to ungrace God's grace.

III. The Cosmic Christ Is the Grace of God

I was visiting a number of years ago and was talking with a mother in her home when a little child was playing around. The child was 4 or 5 years old and I don't remember now what the little fellow did, but she said, "Fella, don't do that. Jesus won't love you."

Well, I thought, I don't know this lady well; this is the first couple of times I've met her, but I'm not going to let that pass. So I watched the little kid and he got involved in something else so he couldn't hear me. I said to her, "Please do not spiritually abuse your child again."

She looked at me kind of astonished.

I said, "That child will never, ever be able to do anything to stop Jesus from loving him. Don't ever spiritually abuse that child again."

God's remarkable, and at times ridiculous grace to us is unconditional. Grace is undeserved. I keep defining grace. "Grace is an irresistible compulsion to give humankind more than they deserve, which springs spontaneously from the boundless generosity and love of God." God has so graced us in Christ but we constantly try to ungrace him. We want to hem that grace in with doctrine and dogma and creedal statements and theological beliefs, and the very essence of Jesus' coming was to set the people free from all of that.

I was preaching at the church I had in Texas. It was a very integrated church. It was racially integrated, economically and vocationally integrated, one of the most integrated congregations I have ever served. It was right near the Texas Women's University. We would often have different people coming. One night I was baptizing. A man came and as he met me at the door—you know they say a lot of things to preachers at the door—he said, "Acts 2:38 says to baptize in the name of Jesus. You didn't do it right."

I had baptized in the name of the Father, the Son, and the Holy Spirit. He said, "Right there it is [finger knocking on the passage]. You didn't baptize in the name of Jesus. You didn't do it right."

You see, that's his formula. If you don't do it by his formula, you don't do it right. And I said to him, "Sir, you don't understand grace." And he says to me, "You don't understand the Bible."

I said, "That's alright, that's alright." You know it's alright when you get that from a visitor who comes to your church. That's not so bad. But when you get it from your denominational hierarchy and when you get it from your ecclesiastical powers, that's a different story. We attempt to ungrace Him constantly. We attempt to ungrace this marvelous, miraculous, beautiful redemptive acquittal grace of God. In Jesus Christ we constantly try to ungrace him.

IV. The Cosmic Christ Is the Truth of God

One of the first churches I served in Texas was a little country church I call quietly to my family "No Hope." It was actually called "New Hope." In that church I invited a person to come and hold a revival. We started on Sunday morning and went through Wednesday night. On Wednesday night he said to that congregation, as he was preaching on John 3:3, where Jesus said to Necodemus, "Except ye be born again," he said to my little congregation, "You know the date of your physical birth. If you do not know the date of your spiritual birth, you've never been born again."

I was just about to get nauseated right there sitting in my church. I said to him at the close of that service, "If this were not the last service scheduled, it would be the last service." I said, "You have created tonight more work for me in the next weeks than I am going to be able to shake a stick at. Do you realize what you have done when you say to a group of people if you can't remember your spiritual birthday, you've never had one?" It is another one of those experiences of un-gracing the grace of God and putting boundaries, putting dogmas, putting creeds around the grace of God that ungraces the grace of God.

Conclusion

Years ago when I was at Travis Avenue Baptist Church while I was still in seminary, I did the children's church. That was in the era of buses. We started growing a bus ministry and we would go all throughout Fort Worth busing in Mexican Americans, African Americans, Native Americans, and any other Americans that would get on that bus. We were bringing in kids from everywhere, and because we couldn't get them back on Sunday night (we didn't run the bus in the evening), we would baptize them in the big church just before the 11 o'clock service. We were growing, so that Dr. Coggins was having to baptize every Sunday morning. One of the deacons said to the associate pastor,

Charles Redmond, "Charles, I'm having a real problem with all of those kids you're running through here. They don't know what they're doing. They don't have any idea what they're doing."

Charles said, "What do you mean?"

He said, "I asked one of them to relate to me his conversion experience and he just stood there looking at me with no expression on his face." And he said, "I want to meet with Reverend Rollins."

I told Charles I'd be delighted to meet with him. "I want to ask him to relate to me the authenticity and historicity of the parthenogenesis of the Lukian account."

Charles said, "Well, he won't have any idea what you're talking about."

I said, "That little kid didn't have any idea what he was talking about: 'Relate to me your conversion experience.' "

We build all these linguistic fences around the grace of God and it ungraces. What would it be like if we just took God at God's word. Jesus who is the Word came, ate with prostitutes, let prostitutes wash his feet, let prostitutes dry his feet with their hair. He went into the homes of sinners, went into the homes of tax collectors, traders, reprobates. The greatest accusal they had of him was that he hobnobbed with the people of the street. What would it be like in our world if we honestly received the grace of God in Jesus Christ as the Mind, and Meaning, and the Glory and the Truth of God and let Grace abound? Maybe we need to start a red word denomination. I like that the more I think about it. But I've lived long enough to know that it wouldn't matter because within just months or years we'd have those who would say, "Those red words don't matter, but these red words do matter."

What matters is grace. And grace is God's Redemptive Acquittal of Us All. Let us fear not to celebrate it, to revel in it and to share it.

Prayer: God, thank you for loving this planet so much that you became one of us, walked among us, loved as no one has ever loved, and died a horrible criminal's death. But the tomb could not contain the glory of God because you yet walk among us even today saying to us, "Be graceful to each other; be graceful to each other." Jesus, help us to be. In Jesus' name, Amen.

Benediction: "And the God of all Grace, who called you to his eternal glory in Christ, after you've suffered a little while, will himself restore you and make you strong, firm, and steadfast. To Him be the power forever and ever." (I Peter 5:10–11, NIV)

✎ Chapter Eight ✎

Grace! It's Radical

TEXT:Luke 15:1–31 (Focus Verses 25–31)

CIT: Jesus used three parables and an angry older brother to illustrate the grace of God.

THESIS: Grace is radical; it does not follow sensible rational guidelines.

PURPOSE: *Major objective:* doctrinal

Specific objective: Through the power of the Holy Spirit, I hope to lead each of us in responding to the radical grace of God.

TITLE: "GRACE! IT'S RADICAL"

INTRODUCTION

OUTLINE:

I.A Radical Shepherd—vv. 3–7

II.A Radical Woman—vv. 8–10

III.A Radical Father—vv. 11–24

IV.A Reasonable Older Brother—vv. 25–31

CONCLUSION

Scripture Reading: Luke 15:25–31 (Focus Verses)

Meanwhile, the older son was in the field. When he came near the house, he heard music and dancing. So he called one of the servants and asked him what was going on. "Your brother has come," he replied, "and your father has killed the fattened calf because he has him back safe and sound."

The older brother became angry and refused to go in. So his father went out and pleaded with him. But he answered his father, "Look! All these years I've been slaving for you and never disobeyed your orders. Yet you never gave me even a young goat so I could celebrate with my friends. But when this son of yours who has squandered your property with prostitutes comes home, you kill the fattened calf for him!"

"My son," the father said, "you are always with me, and everything I have is yours. But we had to celebrate and be glad, because this brother of yours was dead and is alive again; he was lost and is found."

Introduction

Recently I violated one of my principles. That principle is to never open a piece of mail that is addressed to me that does not have a return address and name on it. So, if you want to send me something, give me an address and name—you can lie about the name, it's alright— otherwise, I won't read it. As I violated that principle and read this one, I was reminded again why I made that principle to begin with. If someone is critical of you, you don't know who they are and you don't know what to do about it. In fact, you can do nothing with it. I have apparently insulted someone's religious sensibility. I don't apologize for that. One of the things this person said in the letter was a word I can repeat in this congregation, because it is a word that is part of the text or part of my title. Among other things he said I was radical, one of his or her kinder things. "Radical," Webster says, "is a considerable departure from the traditional." That's Webster's definition of radical. I guess I can accept that. I don't have a problem with accepting that, albeit a departure, a considerable departure, from that which is traditional. That's not a bad definition of grace. In fact, I will say this morning, and

I'll say several times this morning, that grace is radical because it is a considerable departure from the traditional.

One of the things I've said that is so insulting, and I feel so unapologetic about it, that I am going to say it again: God spit in the face of religion and the name of that spit was Jesus Christ. We are so far removed from the Jesus story, the historical circumstance and situation of the Jesus story, we have no idea of how radical this man was. None! It ought to tell us something when religion put him to death because he was radical. We are so far removed from it that we do not have the slightest hint, many of us, of what it means. Radical is a departure, a considerable departure, from the traditional. Believe you me, Jesus was. One of the reasons I've been so radical this summer is that the Christian community has something that the world deeply, deeply needs and we will not give it. We live in a time of ungrace and we have grace, a radical pronouncement of God's affirmation of us, and we want to keep it locked up in ungrace.

Ernest Hemingway knew the life of ungrace experientially. That's why he killed himself, one of the reasons. He writes in one of his books of a story where a father put in the Madrid, Spain, newspaper these words: "Paco," which is a common name in Spain, "Paco, meet me Tuesday at noon in the Montana Hotel parking lot. All is forgiven. Papa." When that father went to the parking lot Tuesday noon, there were 800 Pacos looking for their father.[12] The world lives in ungrace and we will not free it, lose it, and let it be the radical forgiveness, the radical acceptance, the radical affirmation that it is.

I hope you can see in these parables how radical grace really is. It starts out in the fifteenth chapter of Luke, verses 1–3, saying the scribes and the Pharisees are upset. They are talking, murmuring among themselves about this Jesus who claims on the one hand to be God's son and on the other hand he is hobnobbing, eating, and fellowshipping with the sinners, the reprobates of the world. Do you hear how radical this is? They are upset. If he claims to be God's son and he is doing this, it is incongruent. Something is wrong here. They were the representatives of the religious community in Jesus' day. They were condemning him for fellowshipping with the sinners, the have-nots, the people of the streets, the publicans, the tax collectors. So, Jesus tried as best he could with these three parables, I believe, to help them see the radicalness of God who he represented, and the radicalness of grace.

I. A Radical Shepherd

There is a shepherd who has a hundred sheep and one of the sheep strays and is lost in the mountains. The shepherd leaves the ninety-nine and he goes after the one that is lost in the mountains. That, dear friends, is radical. There is not a rational, reasonable shepherd on earth that would leave ninety-nine good healthy sheep and go after one that was dumber than dumb that got lost in the mountains. There's not a shepherd alive that would risk the flock of ninety-nine to go after the one. It's radical. It's ridiculous. It does not make sense. It is not reasonably traditional. Jesus said, that's the way God is. God leaves these ninety-nine safe, secure, and goes after the one that has strayed. You know, sheep are prone to stray.

It is a horrible thing in Scotland and England where they have had to kill all those herds of sheep. I was reading in one journal where a man was so destitute that they had killed his entire flock. The guns were taken out of his house so he would not kill himself. He was so depressed because for four generations his family had been genetically manipulating sheep to get away from their proneness to wander. Isn't it interesting that Isaiah said, "All we like sheep have gone astray, everyone unto his own way"? We are like the sheep. We are prone to wander in our own world of selfish, self-centered, egotistical, I-ness. It is the radical grace of God that pursues us and goes after us. No! No! A shepherd would not have done what Jesus described. Not on your life would that shepherd have left ninety-nine good, healthy sheep and gone after one. But Jesus is saying that's the way God is with us. That's the way God is with you. That's how much God values you. That's what God does. He pursues you until He finds you where you are. It's a radical story of the shepherd.

II. A Radical Woman

Note again, it's a radical story of a woman. Jesus said here is a woman who had ten coins. She loses one of the ten, and she sweeps the house, lights the lamp. She's sweeping and checking everything. She is so anxious about finding this one lost coin. She finds it. And what does she do? She calls in the community and the neighborhood and says, come over to my house and let's have a party. Let's celebrate finding this lost coin. Wonder how much she spent on that party? She spends more on the party celebrating finding this one coin than the one coin was worth. Radical. Radical. She's celebrating because she's happy; she's rejoicing that this one coin has been found. God's grace is that kind of radical with you. It is a considerable departure from the tradition.

III. A Radical Father

Here's that third wonderful parable we have come to know as the prodigal son. I want you to hear the radicalness of it. Here is a younger son who comes to his father and says, "Father, I want my inheritance now." Now, that's pretty cold-blooded. In those days and in that culture, to say to your father, I want my inheritance now was to say to your father, "I wish you dead. I wish you deceased, I want now what I'll get when you do die. Give it to me. I'm out of here." Notice the beginning of the radicalness of the father. The father does not say, "You ingrate! You low-down, sorry, worthless ingrate." That's what I would have done. That's what most of us would have done. The Asian father would not have given him a dime. The Asian father would have said, "If that's what you desire be on your way, but not with my blessing." But he gives this son his share of the inheritance, and he leaves, squanders it, comes to himself, and he comes back. Notice again the radicalness of the father. An Asian father would never have been so common as to be out on the road looking for that son. An Asian father would have never been so common. Not only did he stand out there looking, but when he saw the son he ran after him and fell around him. Totally, absolutely, undignified behavior. Radical. Radical. The son said, make me a servant. I don't deserve anything else. The father says, no. He says to the servants, get some shoes for his feet. Dignity! Get a ring for his hand. Honor! Put a robe on him. He is not a slave, he is not a servant, he is my son who was lost, who was dead, who is found, who is alive. Kill that fatted calf and let us have a party. Radical fatherhood. And Jesus is saying that is the way God is. God does not stand and wait on us when we are repentant and are convicted of our sins and say to us,

"You worthless piece of slime. I'm so glad you've come to yourself." God celebrates. Let's throw a party. This wicked one has returned.

IV. A Reasonable Older Brother

But I want you to see the kicker in this story. There is one who is not radical. There is one who is reasonable. I want to put a name on this reasonable elder brother. This reasonable elder brother's name is Religion. And he is out in the field doing what he is supposed to be doing. He's out in the field doing what he's done every day, working. He hears the music and he comes into the house and he says to the servant, "What's going on? What's happening?"

And the servant says to him, "Your brother's home. Your brother has come home and your daddy's killed the fatted calf and we're about to throw a hoedown." (A calf pickin', I guess you'd say.) And the older brother is angry.

Fred Craddock is a preacher mentor of mine from Atlanta, a brilliant preacher. Fred is very dialogical in communicating with his congregation. I have heard many stories that the congregation gets so caught up in what he is saying that they actually answer him. In this one situation they did. Fred was preaching on this text when he said, "And the elder brother was angry." A woman about midway of the pews in the church said, "He ought to be." She was caught up in it. Her name was Miss Religion because she, too, has been at home doing everything she was supposed to do. This elder brother says to his daddy, "You never killed a fatted calf for me. You never even killed a goat for me to have a party with my friends."

Notice what the father says to him. He says to him, "Everything I have is yours. You've been with me all this time. You've been faithful, and you've lived under the rules and expectations. You've not let me down once. Everything I have is yours. Don't you see it?"

And Mr. Religion says, "No, I don't see it. I don't see it." And that, dear friends, is Religion.

I could put a name on this person because it is a historical person, but I could also put many names on him. But I will call him Mr.

P.K., for preacher kid. Mr. P.K. grew up under a dynamic father who was an immense pulpiteer on most of the impressive boards of his denomination and pastored a large church. From the time Mr. P.K. was small, what he heard from his mama and what he heard from other people was, "If you become half the man your daddy is, you'll be doing wonderfully well." He burned deep within to not be just half the man his daddy was but to surpass his daddy, and to do that, he had to have a call to preach. He got a call to preach. To do that, he had to go to the finest college and university and seminary that his denomination had to offer. He did graduate and he was at the top of his class in all of them. To do that, he had to have a pulpit that was larger than his father's, he had to have bigger buildings, bigger budgets, more baptisms, and he did. And all the while, there was this empty ungrace in his life, that ungraced station of longing to be accepted and affirmed. Finally, one executive female affirmed him. Finally, one loved him and held him. Finally, one came into his life and she took him in and the church put him out. That tragedy of ungraced religious aspiration colors our history from day one.

Listen to this quote from a person whom you will immediately recognize. And he says at the end of his days, "I have spent my life in vain, idle aspiration and continuous prayer, rejected prayer, that my life would somehow benefit." I hope you took that in. For this man was once a US ambassador to Holland. Once a US ambassador to Great Britain. Once a US ambassador to Russia. Once a Secretary of State to the US. Once a US senator. And president of the United States. John and Abigail Adams did such a job with their children that they had to be the moral compass for a universe. That family was so saddled with religious obligation that those that did not become alcoholics became suicide statistics, and John Quincy Adams did his in overachievement. But at the end of his life he cried out, "I spent it in vain, idle aspirations and continuous rejected prayer that I could in some way amount to something."[13] I want to say to you this morning, you ARE enough. You DO amount to something. You don't have to accomplish anything. God loves you.

Conclusion

He was born in 1725. His mother kept him at her knees in the Bible until he was six and she had an untimely death. He was pawned off on relatives who abused him and mistreated him. Finally, as a very young man who could not take that any longer, he left and joined the British navy. There the navy could not contain him. He was AWOL from time to time and finally they put him out. He got in with a Portuguese slave trader. It was said of him at that time that he could cuss for two hours and never use the same word twice. He said on his way to Africa, "I'm going to sin to my fill." The Portuguese slave trader and his family enslaved him. They radically abused him and fed him off the ground. He ate like a dog when he could eat. Thin, emaciated, he finally got away. Got with another British captain and started on a sail ship to England. The captain saw the abilities of this young man and left him in charge one day as he went ashore. This man broke into the rum locker and he and all the crew got "knee-walking" drunk off the rum. The captain hit him in the head and he would have drowned if it had not been for one of the other sailors. Back aboard ship sailing to England, they ran into hard times off the coast of Scotland. They were taking on water. He was down under pumping out water as fast as he could but the ship was going down. There in the belly of that ship his mind went back to the time at his mama's knee. He remembered Ephesians 2:8, "For by grace are you saved through faith." John Newton gave his miserable life to God and became the author of one of the greatest hymns that has every graced our lives. Seventeen fifty-four he wrote "Amazing Grace." Whether you are in the midst of a religious endeavor trying to do your very best and feeling so ungraced, or whether you are out in the periphery of life living, as some would say, sinfully, wherever you are, God's grace says to you radically, "I love you and I want you to know you are my child. My love for you and my acceptance of you IS amazing, radically amazing." Amen.

Prayer: Oh Lord, help us. Help us to get just a small sense of how much you love us. Help us to get a sense of why Jesus came and lived, took our sins upon himself and died. In Jesus' name, Amen.

❧ Chapter Nine ❧

Grace! It's Lavish

TEXT: John 12:1–8

CIT: In a lavish act of grace, Mary anointed Jesus' feet with a pint of very valuable perfume.

THESIS: An act of grace brings into the world something permanently precious which time cannot ever take away.

PURPOSE: *Major objective:* Devotional

Specific objective: Through the power of the Holy Spirit, I hope to lead each of us   in giving and receiving grace.

TITLE: "GRACE! IT'S LAVISH"

INTRODUCTION

OUTLINE:

I. A Lavish Act of Grace—v. 3

II. A Lamentable Act of Ungrace—v. 5

CONCLUSION

Scripture Reading: John 12:1–8

Six day before Passover, Jesus arrived at Bethany, where Lazarus lived, whom Jesus had raised from the dead. Here a dinner was given in Jesus' honor. Martha served, while Lazarus was among those reclining at the table with him. Then Mary took about a pint of pure nard, an expensive perfume; she poured it on Jesus' feet and wiped his feet with her hair. And the house was filled with the fragrance of the perfume.

But one of his disciples, Judas Iscariot, who was later to betray him, objected, "Why wasn't this perfume sold and the money given to the poor? It was worth a year's wages." He did not say this because he cared about the poor but because he was a thief; as keeper of the money bag, he used to help himself to what was put into it.

"Leave her alone," Jesus replied. "It was meant that she should save this perfume for the day of my burial. You will always have the poor among you, but you will not always have me."

Introduction

We have a beautiful national illustration of what I've been trying to say, and will be trying to say all summer. It happened this past week. It was in Chicago. It actually happened in April; it was reported this past week (July 2001). A waitress by the name of Gallagher is waiting upon this gentleman's table. In conversation he happens to find out she's a single mother and does not have personal transportation. She rides the bus to and from work. His tab is $60.00. How many of you have heard this? He leaves her an $11,000.00 tip. Legit! He's not wanting to father her next child. This is totally legit. He leaves her a tip of $11,000.00. Grace is lavish. I want you to know that was an act of grace. Undeserved. She may be good at waiting on tables but she's not that good. Underserved, unmerited favor. A lavish expression of grace. Grace is lavish.

I. A Lavish Act of Grace

Webster says in defining lavish, it means to squander. Also, in that definition it says to bestow with profusion; it is a superfluity of; an abundance of. Grace is lavish. Let's look at a biblical lavish experience of grace.

Jesus has once said that the foxes have dens and the birds of the air have nests but the son of man has no place to lay his head. For the last years of his life Jesus was an itinerant preacher, much like our old going from community to community, house to house preaching and teaching, staying with whomever would invite him in. One of those families that habitually invited him in was Lazarus, and Mary and Martha, his two sisters. Often when Jesus was in and around Bethany, he stayed with this family. According to John's gospel, this event is right after he resurrects Lazarus from the dead. That may have had something to do with the lavish act of grace that we have in our text. However it was, they are there probably again in the home of Mary, Martha, and Lazarus, and unlike us today, they did not eat sitting upright. They were in a reclining position around a very low table twelve or fourteen inches off the floor. They would recline and eat. There, after the meal, Mary, the sister of Martha and Lazarus, opens up a pint of extremely expensive perfume. She pours it upon Jesus' feet and then she wipes off the excess with her hair. I want you to see grace as extravagance in this act. I'll talk about him in a moment, but Judas slashes out, "Why did we not prevent this? That was a year's wages." So here Mary is taking a year's wages worth of perfume and anointing Jesus' feet. It is a lavish, almost squanderous act. An act of profusion, superfluity, abundance there on Jesus' feet.

O Henry, an English writer, is superb at short stories. In one of his short stories, "The Gift of the Magi," he talks about a young couple, Della and Jim. They are an American, blue collar couple. They have very little; they work very hard. It's the day before Christmas and Della has $1.87. She wants to purchase Jim a present but she has nothing of worth. Of course, he wants to reciprocate but he has nothing of worth, except . . . Jim has a gold watch that his grandfather gave his father that his father gave to him. That's really his only valuable possession. Della on the other hand has a valuable possession. She has hair that is so long and thick and beautiful that it almost serves as a robe. So the day before Christmas, she goes out and has her hair shorn and she sells it for $20.00. She buys Jim a leather backing and a gold chain for his pocket watch that was an inheritance.

Jim comes in that night and looks at her and he is in shock. Not because she is not beautiful. She's even more beautiful than she was before. But he is in shock at the situation. Della understands as he takes out a gift of turquoise hair combs, a set, with pearl edges for her beautiful hair. That's grace. That is grace. Motivated and fostered by a deep sense of love. That is the kind of extravagant grace that is displayed at this moment. Mary lavishes this act of grace on Jesus. I want you to notice also the humility of this act of grace, as it is with many acts of grace. It was customary in that day that one anoint the head. Remember the twenty-third Psalm? "And he annointeth my head with oil, my cup runneth over." To be blessed, to be graced, one would have one's head anointed. Mary does not anoint Jesus' head. She anoints his feet. That lowliest part of the human anatomy that constantly and continually makes contact with the humus, the earth. That part of the human anatomy that gets dirty and dusty walking the country roads in and around Jerusalem and the bare cobble streets. She does not presume and anoint his head. Lowly, she's down on her knees and anoints his feet. It's an extravagant act of grace. It's a humble act of grace. It's also an extremely unselfconscious act of grace. Why would I say so? In that time when a woman was seen outside with her hair unbound, unbraided, loose, she was considered a woman of the street, a prostitute. In public, Mary takes her hair down and dries Jesus' feet with her glory, as I Corinthians says. "Her glory." See the humility, the unselfconsciousness, unawareness of this act. A beautiful act, a lavish act of grace. It points us I believe to the lavish acts of grace of God because Jesus is so moved by it. This underserved movement of Mary, lavishing this expensive gift upon him. To me, it is very, very deeply connected to what God did in God's grace—the extravagance of God's grace to us in Jesus Christ, the emptying of himself and the coming to earth and taking on the form, the likeness of human flesh and becoming one of us. In the humility of that and going to the cross, the death of a criminal, laying down his life on our behalf, for your sins and for mine. It is the unselfconsciousness of that, the awesome humility of that cross. This gift I believe, this act of grace, is very much connected to the grace of Christ.

II. A Lamentable Act of Ungrace

In context and in contrast of that lavish act of grace, I want you to see the lamentable act of ungrace. Judas cries out, "Why was this not stopped?" This was a year's wages. It could have been given to the poor. John's very clear about that. Judas doesn't have any concern for the poor. Judas was a zealot, meaning his one all-consuming purpose was to see Israel throw off the yoke of Roman rule and see the Messiah, Jesus Christ, whom he believed to be in the beginning, throw off that yoke of rule and for Israel to once again become a nation. That was Judas' burning desire and that money could have been used to buy swords, arms for the rebellion.

I want us to see in this moment a kinship between the ungrace of Judas and the grace of Mary—a picture of grace and the un-gracing that the institutional church often does. I want us also to contrast that with Martha, Mary's sister, who I also believe symbolically represents the church. Now, I can hear some of you thinking, "Gene, you've kind of been beating up on the church the last few weeks." Well, let me settle something for you. I am unapologetically a churchman. In October, it will be 34 years of my life I've dedicated to the church. But I am not one of those Americans or churchmen who believe Love It or Leave It. You know what that says on the back of a car, that bumper snicker? It says, "Love America uncritically or leave her." I love her unapologetically but I am not nor have ever been uncritical. I'll be critical of her with her politics and her policies and her lack of benevolence until the day they walk by and say, "He finally shut up." I long ago made the commitment that I am a churchman. If I get outside the church and throw rocks, they will only disregard me and invalidate my voice. No, I am committed to the church but not uncritically. I am one of her greatest critics and I'll continue to be. I'm the greatest critic of our own denomination and I'll continue to be. For I think now for several decades the Presbyterian church has walked down a road that is nothing but a dead end road and we have spent enormous amounts of money and enormous amounts of time missing the mission God called us to do. Let me give you a definition of the mission of the church that I'll put with any mission of the church. And it is this: the church's one and only mission is to dispense the grace of God. That's all we've been called to do—to dispense, to share, to promote the grace of God. When we start dibbling and dabbling in anything else, closing the doors to this particular person because of race, creed, gender, color or sexual orientation, then we are down a road that is blind and dead end and it will not do anything but cost us like it has.

I don't know if you are aware of it, but Presbyterian rolls have declined since 1983 like a snowball down a hill. One of the reasons for that is we've lost our mission. We want to argue and fight about who can be included fully in the church. It's not just in my church, it's in your church and it has a long history. For a long while the Blacks could not have full fellowship within the church. We couldn't even educate them. Then it was the women. And it still is women in some churches. Some mainline denominations still do not accept women fully in their church. They cannot be ordained as deacon or elder. They cannot be ordained as minister. Here now for the last 20 years, Presbyterian churches have gone to seed over whether or not we are going to ordain homosexuals. We've lost our mission. We're living out our existence in the land of ungrace. The bottom line truth is not any of us deserve anything. To be recipients of God's favor is to be recipients of God's grace. We best not start closing the doors to anyone.

The mission of the church is to share God's grace, dispense God's grace. That's all, nothing more. Here is a beautiful example of what Mary is doing. In Luke's account of this experience there in the home, Martha is one of those duty bound, and I'm not saying this is bad. Thank God some folks are duty bound—they get things done. But here is Martha getting everything ready in the kitchen and getting everything worked up. She's just working, working, working. There's Mary seated at the feet of Jesus listening to his every word. Martha comes in and says, "Lord, don't you care, aren't you aware, she's left me to do all the work?" Picture that. That's a conflict between the ungrace of the church and the grace. Jesus says, "Mary has chosen the best gift and it will not be taken from her. Leave her alone." He says the same thing to Judas. "Leave her alone. She is dispensing grace." And I love that verse in our text. It says the whole house was filled with the fragrance of the perfume. I want to say to you that our environment will be filled with the fragrance of our acts of grace to each other as we dispense, disburse, share, and promote the grace of God. The world will not be the same. We do not live in a world of grace. We live in a world of ungrace. Quid pro quo. No pain, no gain. You know, if you don't work, you don't get anything back. It's that quid pro quo all through our society. We're not a society of grace. What would it be like if we graced each other, if that was a constant awareness of ours, to live out God's grace and to be dispensers of God's grace to each other?

Coming back from Columbia this week, I came a different route than I usually take. It was a little after lunch and I was hungry. I stopped into this country diner, one I'd never stopped in before. But I love to go into these places. The place is half full of blue collar workers, mud on their boots, and they are eating with their caps on, and I like that. They sit around the table cussing. That's just not a normal environment for me. I get into those kinds of environments and just love it. They push back from the table after they eat and have another cup of coffee and tea and smoke a cigarette or something. Most of the places I go to would run them off if they did that. But the waitress did a good job, was efficient, but had a real dental problem. I know she didn't have the money to have her teeth fixed. With this other example in the back of my mind, I thought I would just love to lavish upon her the roll of bills and a card from my dentist and say, "Darling, you've done a marvelous job and you could be so much more presentable, just go get your teeth fixed with this money." I lavished her with a tip but it was just a dollar more than what I usually give. But what would it be like if we had those kind of examples of gracing each other in the workplace, in the place of recreation? Can you imagine gracing each other in our homes? "Oh now, don't talk about that, preacher. Don't start meddling with my wife and me." But what would it be like if we lived in that constant, "I don't want to be graced; I want to be the dispenser of grace. I want to share grace because it means I'm going to be graced more in order to be more graceful."

Conclusion

Paul Harvey used to do those "Rest of the Story" commentaries. This is one of those stories. A child is born without ears. He has holes in the head and has eardrums. He can hear, but there are no outside attachments as we have them. In the early years of school, that's no problem. He goes to school. He starts socially adjusting and everything else without any problems, and his mother tries to keep his hair a little bit long to cover up that the ear holes. So, he really doesn't have a bad problem. But you know when you get into those middle school years, children are the most cruel people in the entire world. If anything is different within you, they point it out, not privately and tactfully, but publicly. So, he was harassed and harangued continually about having no ears. The doctors, surgeons, and cosmetic people kept telling the parents that there was nothing they could do until he got past the growing stage. Then, with ear donations, they could surgically attach the ears. However, they could not do it now. So, he finishes high school, goes to college, and does well while he gets an engineering degree. He goes to Europe in his first engineering job. His father calls him and tells him that his mother has died. Earlier, between his high school and his college years, he had received ears from a donor. He had two beautiful, functional ears. That's all he ever knew. When he came back from Europe to his mother's funeral, in a private meeting with his father in the funeral home, the father reached down and pulled his mother's hair aside. Her ears had been removed and donated to her son. That is grace. That is the kind of grace that would turn our world right side up. That is the kind of grace that the church must become aware of. That is the kind of grace we must become dispensers of. Grace: God's unmerited, undeserved blessings.

Prayer: Lord, you tell us in your word that the act of Mary, wherever the Gospel is preached, will be remembered. We have remembered her lavish act of grace this day, and hopefully it has helped us see your lavish act of Jesus Christ coming and living and dying for us. Also, Lord, I hope it has helped us to see that we need to be living as recipients and dispensers of your marvelous and amazing grace. In Jesus' name, Amen.

๑ Chapter Ten ๑

Grace! It's Impartial

TEXT:Matthew 20:1–16

CIT: The landowner gave the same amount of pay to the worker who worked an hour as he did to the worker who worked all day.

THESIS: Grace is God's to give any way God chooses to give it.

PURPOSE: *Major objective:* evangelistic

Specific objective: Through the power of the Holy Spirit, I hope to lead each of us in responding to God's gift of grace.

TITLE: "GRACE! IT'S IMPARTIAL"

INTRODUCTION

OUTLINE:

I.Grace for the Worthy—vv. 1–4

II.Grace for the Not-So-Worthy—v. 5

III.Grace for the Unworthy—vv. 6–7

CONCLUSION

Scripture Reading: Matthew 20:1–16

For the kingdom of heaven is like a landowner who went out early in the morning to hire men to work in his vineyard. He agreed to pay them a denarius for the day and sent them into his vineyard.

About the third hour, he went out and saw others standing in the marketplace doing nothing. He told them, "You also go and work in my vineyard, and I will pay you whatever is right," so they went.

He went out again about the sixth hour and the ninth hour and did the same thing. About the eleventh hour, he went out and found still others standing around. He asked them, "Why have you been standing here all day long doing nothing?"

"Because no one had hired us," they answered.

He said to them, "You also go and work in vineyard."

When evening came, the owner of the vineyard said to his foreman, "Call the workers and pay them their wages, beginning with the last ones hired and going on to the first."

The workers who were hired about the eleventh hour came and each received a denarius. So when those came who were hired first, they expected to receive more. But each one of them also received a denarius. When they received it, they began to grumble against the landowner. "These men who were hired last worked only one hour," they said, "and you have made them equal to us who have borne the burden of the work and the heat of the day."

But he answered one of them, "Friend, I am not being unfair to you. Didn't you agree to work for a denarius? Take your pay and go, I want to give the man who was hired last the same as I gave you. Don't I have the right to do what I want with my own money? Or are you envious because I am generous?"

So the last will be first, and the first will be last.

Introduction

This parable of the kingdom is one of those parables that has strong support for what the historical theologians call the criteria of "dissimilarity." It is dissimilar because it is not likely at all that the church would have allowed this to remain in the Scripture had there not been strong historical evidence that Jesus said it. It is contradictory. It is cross-grained to life experience. It is dissimilar. Of all of Jesus' parables, this is the least liked parable of them all. For some of us, it is our favorite. But for most of us, it is not liked and in fact, in relationship to some, despised. Let's look at it.

Jesus says, "The kingdom of God is like . . ." Now that should throw up a red flag for us and call our attention, arrest us right at that point. The kingdom of God. The kingdom is in the New Testament more than 70 different places. So anytime there is a word or phrase that occurs that often, it bears looking seriously at it. So what is this kingdom that is being referred to here and referred to so very, very often? In Matthew's Gospel, it is recorded that Jesus said in the sixth chapter, verse 33, "Seek ye first the kingdom of God and God's righteousness and all these other things will be added unto you." In other words the Matthew passage is saying that if there is a priority in our lives, our lives will take on a focus and a meaning that is unique. The first priority is to seek the kingdom of God. When that is paramount in our lives, everything else falls into place according to this passage. In the first chapter of Mark it is recorded that Jesus' very first sermon was, "Repent, for the kingdom of God is at hand." So it is to be sought after above everything else. It was Jesus' first sermon. Are you aware that we repeated it a few moments ago? For those churches that are liturgical enough to repeat the Lord's Prayer every Sunday morning as we do as Presbyterians, we pray every Sunday morning, "Thy kingdom come . . ." Did we not pray it? We pray it every Sunday morning. Then if it takes priority in our worship, in our everyday worship, it's a part of our collective worship. Jesus said seek it first above all else. What is it? In the seventeenth chapter of Luke it is defined clearer than you will find it anywhere else. Jesus said according to Luke's' Gospel, the seventeenth chapter, "the kingdom of God cannot be seen. The kingdom of God is within you." The kingdom of God is the rule and the reign of God in one's life. So, when Jesus said the kingdom has come when he came, he was stating it clearly. The kingdom has come to live within you. It is the rule and reign of God. When we pray every Sunday morning, "Thy kingdom come on Earth as it is in Heaven, " we are saying, "may the rule and reign of God be as clear and concise here on this earth as it is with our Creator in Heaven." The kingdom of God is within you. So, Jesus says in this parable, the kingdom of God, the rule and the reign of God within you is likened unto this.

I. Grace for the Worthy

It is astonishing that the stories Jesus tells are so simple, so clear, and so expressive of the life around him. It's probably the grape harvesting season, and when the grapes get ready you better be ready. They don't wait, just like our peaches in South Carolina. When the peach is at its peak, you best be there to pick it. Someone has to be there to pick. It's not going to wait on you. It's harvest time. Be ready. So Jesus said the kingdom of God is like this. This landowner goes out at six o'clock in the morning and he goes down to the labor pool. Every community has a labor pool. Camden may have more than one, but the one I know of is there at Dusty Bend where the old hardware store used to be. I think they hang around next to Trader's now. But there is a labor pool there. You can go pick people up to work as day laborers. Every town has one of these places in them. You go and offer them so much and they will work for so much. So Jesus said the landowner goes down to the labor market at six o'clock in the morning and he asks, "Would you like to work for a denarius?" And they say yes. That is a standard day's pay. It was a silver coin, 3.8 grams of silver with Tiberius', the Roman Emperor's, insignia on it and minted in 268 b.c. It was a standard day's pay. It was like our hourly wage today. So Jesus said to these workers, "Would you work for a day for a denarius?" They said, "Sure." That's standard pay; we'll give you standard pay. So, he takes a load of them to the field at six o'clock in the morning and they start to work.

II. Grace for the Not-So-Worthy

It's not enough workers. The grapes have got to be picked. So the landowner goes back to the labor market again at nine o'clock and he sees some people not working. He say, "Would you like to work for me today?" And they say, yes, and he says alright. "Let's go to the field. I'll pay you what's right." So, at nine o'clock he takes another load of workers to the field. He goes back at noon and there are others still standing around. He loads them up another load at noon and takes them to the field. He goes back at three o'clock. Does the same thing and takes another load to the field.

III. Grace for the Unworthy

He goes back at five, one hour before sunset. One hour yet left to work. And he takes another load and takes them to the field. They work one hour.

At the close of the day—they paid every day—the landowner instructs the foreman, "Start paying the last hired first and pay them a denarius," a day's work. Those who came at the eleventh hour, five o'clock, worked one hour got one day's pay. Those who came at three o'clock worked three hours and got one denarius, one day's pay. Those who came at twelve got a day's pay. And those who had been working since six o'clock that morning came to the paymaster and said, "Whoa. Wait a minute. This is not right. We have been here since six o'clock this morning bearing the heat of the day, picking the fruit of the vine and there are others who came at five o'clock, worked one hour, and when we watched them get paid a whole denarius for one hour we thought, 'Wow, what are we going to get when he comes down to us?' You're giving us the same pay you gave them. That's not right."

And the landlord said, "Did I not offer you a denarius?"

"Yes."

"Did you not get it?"

"Yes, but it's not right. We worked all day long and we get a coin. They worked one hour and get a coin? It's not right. There's something wrong with this picture."

If you miss everything else I say, don't miss this. Devine and cosmic grace is God's, and God can give it to whomever God chooses to give to and it's none of your business. That's what the foreman should have said. Well, in fact he did. He said it kinder than I would have said it.

"Look, friend. Did I break my contract with you?

"No."

"Is this not my money?"

"Yes."

"Then can't I give it to whomever I choose to give it to?"

"But it still ain't right. We still don't like it."

Here I've been in the church all my life. I'm eighty-five years old. I love Jesus. I've tithed my income. I've supported missionaries. I've gone to services when I didn't feel like it. I've dragged my sick body out of bed on Sunday morning when all my neighbors were sleeping in. I went to church when the rest of them were out on the lake fishing. I've given Jesus all my life, and now the end, I see fisherman Joe that didn't give him squat and it ain't right. It ain't right. I don't like it.

Cosmic and divine grace is God's, and it's God's to give to whomever God chooses to give it to.

When I'm preaching a series of sermons like I am now, I like to read from my devotional time the lectionary because quite often I am preaching the lectionary. The Christian calendar developed the lectionary many years ago. It's A, B and C, and when you read these texts, A-year, B-year, and C-year, by the time you get to the third year, you've gone through the Old Testament and New Testament and the Wisdom literature. So when I'm not preaching some of those texts, I like to read them as devotion. The day that Timothy McVeigh was executed by our government, the text was on forgiveness. I read it hurriedly, flippantly, tried to put it away, tried to deny and repress this other thought that was rambling through my mind and hitting me between the eyes and I could not. Forgiveness, God's grace, Timothy McVeigh, who killed 168 people, nineteen of whom were innocent infants and children, whose last request, but I think he withdrew it, was to have his ashes scattered over the city he devastated. But I think he withdrew it. And I asked, "Is there any grace? Surely, it's not right! Is there any grace for the killer of 168 people, 19 of who are babies? Is there forgiveness?" And then I realized what was really important. Is there forgiveness in my heart? Can I pray for him? Never had. Can I pray for him? Can I hold a sense of grace? Can I forgive him? Then my mind just goes crazy. And I thought of Adolf Hitler in that bunker in Berlin in 1945, the killer of six million-plus Jews. Is there any grace in that bunker? Is there any mercy in that bunker? No, can't be. It's not right! Is there? You see why we don't like this parable? You see why you so identify whether you'll admit it or not with those who started to work at six o'clock in the morning. You'd be right there beside them, I'd be right there beside them, saying, "Whoa, don't I get a little bonus here? Come on. It's not right. It's not fair."

Grace is not fair. It is not fair. It is not fair that Saturday morning while eating breakfast I experience natural grace in seeing the beauty of that eagle when there are millions of people who will never see anything like that and greater millions that could not care about something like that because they are scratching out enough food just today to live. There's nothing fair about grace. Nothing. We start to work at six o'clock and they start at five, you're going to pay us equal pay, it's not right.

Grace is not fair. That's the part of grace we do not like. We do not like its impartiality. It feels unfair to us. It is unfair!

If you have never read Will Campbell, you need to read him. You owe it to yourself. You at least need to read *Brother of a Dragonfly*. Maybe you need to read *Forty Acres and a Goat*. I love that one. Will Campbell is a Southern Baptist minister born in Mississippi who graduated from Yale divinity school. He was always a little bookish for Mississippi children, always kind of felt like an outsider. When he graduated from Yale divinity school, he went back to the University of Mississippi as a religious director. It was in the 1960s when Will's heart was with those who were pushing equal rights—integration. The school kicked him out. He stayed on struggling for equal rights and equal opportunity. A young man came down from Harvard divinity school, Jonathan Daniels, 26 years of age. Will worked with him, supported him, was his mentor, loved him. Another man in that little book, J. D. East, a newspaper reporter, says to Will, "Will, define your theology for me in ten words. Ten words. That's all you can have. Define religion, define your commitment, define theology, define religious Christian faith in ten words. Ten words. That's all you've got." He kept pushing Will. I'm going to use a word here, but don't blame me for the word I'm quoting. And don't even blame me for choosing to quote the word because it is in the Bible. It's in the Bible three times, two in the Old Testament, and one in the New Testament. If you don't believe it look at Hebrews 12:8. And J. D. pushes Will to define his theology in ten words. And Will says this: "We're all bastards, but God loves us anyway."

J. D. says, "That's just eight words. I'm going to give you another chance. You can use ten."

Will thought about it and said, "No, I'm going to stick with my eight."

Jonathan Daniels was arrested for picketing a white candy store and was put into jail. Will Campbell helped to get his bond. He got out and went to a pay phone on a Mississippi street to call and get a ride. Thomas Coleman, a deputy, stopped a block away, walked up to Jonathan Daniels, 26-year-old Harvard graduate, and shot him in the stomach with a shotgun. Killed him right there. Will Campbell had lost a dear friend and was in a puddle of tears. J. D. said to him, "Will, tell me about your theology in relationship to Jonathan Daniels? Was Jonathan Daniels a bastard?"

And Joe, Will's brother, tries to stop him but he won't be stopped.

He said, "Tell me, Will."

Will said, "Jonathan, Daniel was the sweetest, precious, caring young man I have ever met in the world."

"Was he a bastard, Will?

Will said, "Yes, it means he was a sinner. Yes, he was a sinner."

He said, "How about Thomas Coleman, the deputy who shot him? Will, is he a bastard?"

Will had no problem saying yes to that question.

Then J. D., smart-aleck reporter that he was, but deeply insightful, shook Will Campbell to his knees. He said, "Will, which of the two bastards did God love the most?"

Will Campbell started sobbing, screaming, and his sobs and his screams went to laughter. His laughter went to shouts. He said, "I thought I was having a psychotic break." And the greatest realization of his ministry came when Will Campbell said, "He loves them both equally or there is no Gospel. He loves them both or there is no grace." We have no message if God's grace is not there for the Jonathan Danielses and the Thomas Colemans of our lives.[14]

Conclusion

I was closing out a unit of clinical pastoral education at Kershaw prison last Monday. I was waiting on my first student to come and go over his evaluation with me, and a chaplain clerk came out to my little office and said, "Chaplain, there is someone who needs to see a chaplain and Ralph's in training in Columbia. Could you see him?"

I said, "Sure. I might as well work while I'm waiting." So in a few moments he brought the inmate into my office. An aged white man. I could tell he was broken by the penal system. I could see the scars of incarceration on his face, literally, and a disabled arm.

He said to me, "Chaplain, I'm maxing out in two months. I want to go home to Houston. Can I make it?"

I said, "You've been here how long?"

He said, "Since '66. Shot three people. I'm maxing out in two months. Can I make it?"

Did you hear what he was asking? Is there grace for me? Can I leave this graceless place and hope, expect to find grace? I took him by his scarred hand and we prayed. Deep within me was rumbling over the question I posed for us this morning. Can there really be grace? Here's an eleventh-hour worker. Is there grace? There is. There must be whether we like it or not. There must be.

Prayer: Oh, Lord, we get so hooked on fairness and justice. Some of us who toiled, worked, sometimes work when we wish we could play, but out of duty, out of ungrace, we work when we wanted to play. We see those who enter the kingdom of heaven who played all their lives, except the eleventh hour. We don't like it. God help us to see your grace and to want your grace to be shattered, scattered, poured out upon everyone because grace is undeserved and unmerited, divine favor. May it be so, in Jesus' name, Amen.

∽ *Chapter Eleven* ∾

Grace! It's Compassion

TEXT:Matthew 23:1–39 (Focus Verses 37–39)

CIT: Jesus accused the organized religion of his day of being without grace and compassion.

THESIS: We must let go of a religion of ungrace and embrace a spirituality of grace and compassion.

PURPOSE: *Major objective:* ethical/actional

Specific objective: Through the power of the Holy Spirit, I hope to lead each of us into a commitment of grace and compassion.

TITLE: "GRACE! IT'S COMPASSION"

INTRODUCTION

OUTLINE:

I.Woe to You Religion of Ungrace—vv. 13–34

II.Wow to You Spirituality of Grace and Compassion—v. 37

CONCLUSION

Scripture Reading: Matthew 23:37–39 (Focus Verses)

Then Jesus said to the crowds and to his disciples: "The teachers of the law and the Pharisees sit in Moses' seat. So you must obey them and do everything they tell you. But do not do what they do, for they do not practice what they preach. They tie up heavy loads and put them on men's shoulders, but they themselves are not willing to lift a finger to move them. Everything they do is done for men to see: They make their phylacteries wide and the tassels of their prayer shawls long; they love the place of honor at banquets and the most important seats in the synagogues; they love to be greeted in the marketplaces and to have men call them 'Rabbi.'

"O Jerusalem, Jerusalem, you who kill the prophets and stone those sent to you, how often I have longed to gather your children together, as a hen gathers her chicks under her wings, but you were not willing. Look, your house is left to you desolate. For I tell you, you will not see me again until you say, 'Blessed is he who comes in the name of the Lord.' "

Introduction

Our text this morning is the 23rd chapter of Matthew. It should be considered in its totality of all 39 verses. It needs to be considered as a whole. You are aware, of course, that when the Scriptures were written, they didn't have chapters and verses. We did that to them so we could remember them and remember where they were. It does distract from the text at times. This particular text is problematic, deeply problematic. It is problematic because of two sources, at least two sources. On the one hand Jesus, mild, meek, and lowly, is pronouncing seven woes on the Scribes and Pharisees. One problem is that many people who come to this text have no idea who these people were. As you know, I did not grow up in the church. I'm not a product of the church. I came to the text as an adult. Remembering how meek and mild I had read about Jesus to this point, I was astonished and perplexed. I wondered who in the world these people were that Jesus could call them snakes, whitewashed graves, unclean dishes, persons who are going to Hell before anyone else goes. I tried in my limited, novice, uneducated way at that time in my life to find out who these people were. I realized that they were the religious leaders of Jesus' day. The Pharisees were the deep proponents, perpetuators of the law of Moses, and the Scribes were the caretakers of the temple and temple sacrifices. Both of these two groups of people represented organized religion in Jesus' day. In essence, they were the church, although the church was not in existence at that time.

The other problem is a different kind of problem. Mary C. Boys, in her book entitled *Has God Only Got One Blessing?* points this out very clearly and poignantly. She says this is one of the texts that the Christian church has used to browbeat the Jews. Jews are responsible for the killing of God, and this is one of those texts where Jews are deeply denounced.[15] Well, that's not true. The Scribes and the Pharisees made up only a very small percentage of the Jewish nation at that time, an extremely small percentage of the Jewish population. Yet, Jesus is rather hard on this small segment of the Jewish people. It is not a denunciation of the entire Jewish culture and world. So this text has two problems based upon ignorance. One is the lack of knowledge and the other is knowledge that is not accurate.

I want to read the text in a way you've probably never heard it before. I want us to think about it in that fashion. As always, I never ask you to agree with me. I don't care whether you agree with me or not. That matters absolutely zero to me. What does matter to me is whether or not you understand what I'm saying and that you have some understanding why I'm saying the ridiculous stuff that I say. If you have a little bit of that understanding, I'm okay with that. I seek to be understood, not agreed with.

To set the stage, Buddha was a Hindu and he never, ever intended to structure something known as Buddhism. At least history doesn't show it that way. Rather, his intention was to revitalize and reform Hinduism. That was his goal.

The same is true with Jesus. You do not find any historical evidence that Jesus ever intended to launch a new religion. Not at all. Jesus was a Jew, a good Jew. Jesus' desire was to revitalize and reform Judaism. There is no historical evidence that Jesus' desire was to start a new religion. He wanted to bring new life to Judaism.

There is no evidence historically that Martin Luther intended to start a new movement known as the Protestant Reformation. Martin Luther was a Catholic and he wanted to revitalize and reform Catholicism. He had no intent of ever starting Protestantism.

So, what happened with these great leaders and great people with awesome magnetism and charisma, who attempted one thing which turned into something else? I personally do not believe that Christ ever intended to make a religion. I personally believe the darkest day of the evolving church, the darkest day in Christianity, came in 325 when Constantine made Christianity the state religion. It was the darkest day in my opinion of the movement from its very beginning.

I. Woe to You Religion of Ungrace

Jesus was an apocalyptic prophet, a denouncer of ungrace religion. He was a denouncer of religion that was not filled with grace, mercy, and compassion. He fell right in line with a lot of the other prophets who had taught before him and preached before him the same message that he was attempting to preach. Listen to the prophet Isaiah, chapter one, verses 13–15. He says, "Stop bringing your meaningless offerings. Your incense is detestable to me. Your new moons, Sabbath, and convocations. I cannot bear your evil assemblies." Boy, wouldn't that be something. Here we are in church on Sunday morning and a voice comes from heaven saying, "I cannot bear your evil assembly." Wow, that would scare you. "Your new moon festivals and your appointed feast, my soul hates. They have become a burden to me. I am weary of them. When you spread your hands in prayer, I'll hide my eyes from you. Even if you offer many prayers, I will not listen."

Listen to the prophet again in chapter 29 of Isaiah, verse 13. "These people come near to me with their mouth and honor me with their lips but their hearts are far from me. Their worship of me is made up of only rules taught by men." What are the prophets saying? They are in opposition to a religion that is of ritual, of word and not deed, of ritual and not mercy, and not grace. Listen to Micah, 6th chapter, verses 6–8, another prophet. "With what shall I come before the Lord and bow down before Thee Exalted God? Shall I come before Him with burnt offerings, with calves a year old? Would the Lord be pleased with thousand of rams, with ten thousand rivers of oil?"

That was the Jewish religion and now he speaks to the pagan religion. "Shall I offer my firstborn for the transgression of the fruit of my body? For the sin of my soul? He has shown you oh man what is good. And what does the Lord require of you? To act justly, to love mercy, and to walk humbly with you, God." There is the contract between ungrace religion and a spirituality that is grace and compassion.

Now hear this reading of the twenty-third chapter of Matthew. I want to read it to you like you have never heard it. You can leave here saying I have done an injustice to the Scripture if you want to. That's okay. I hope you will understand what I am saying.

Verse 13: "Woe to you, ungrace religion. You hypocrites. You shut the kingdom of heaven in men's faces. You yourselves do not enter, nor will you let those enter who are trying."

Verse 15: "Woe to you, ungrace religion. You hypocrites. You travel over land and sea to win a single convert, and when he becomes one, you make him twice as much the son of hell as you are." Wow.

Verses 16–17: "Woe to you, ungrace religion. You blind fools. If someone swears by the temple, it means nothing. If someone swears by the gold of the temple, he is bound by his oath. Which is greater—the gold or the temple that makes the gold sacred?"

Verse 23: "Woe to you, ungrace religion. You give a tenth of your spices, mint, dill, cumin, but you have neglected the more important matters of law, justice, mercy, faithfulness."

Verse 25: "Woe to you, ungrace religion. You hypocrites. You clean the outside of the cup and the dish, but inside they are full of greed and self-indulgence."

Verse 27: "Woe to you, ungrace religion. You hypocrites. You are like whitewashed tombs. You look beautiful on the outside, but on the inside you are full of dead men's bones and everything unclean."

Verse 29: "Woe to you, ungrace religion. You hypocrites. You blind Pharisees. You build tombs for the prophets, decorate the graves of the righteous, and say, 'If we lived back in the days of our forefathers, we would not have taken part in the shedding of the blood of the prophets.' You snakes, you brood of vipers. How will you escape from being condemned to Hell?"

That is a picture of a religion lacking in grace, lacking in mercy: a religion that builds temples and synagogues and churches and spends its time and energy in rules and regulation without any show of mercy and of grace. Jesus denounces that kind of religion. I want to say to you, as we have said throughout these many, many years together on the lake, it's not our goal, it's not my goal to make Presbyterians of you. I don't care whether you ever become a Presbyterian or not. I don't care if you are Baptist or not. Methodist or not. I really don't care what you are in relationship to titles. I don't care whether you call yourself Christian. I don't care whether you call yourself Protestant. I don't care whether you call yourself Catholic. I don't care whether you call yourself Hindu. I don't care whether you call yourself Buddhist. You know what I care about and what I have been hammering at all summer? Are we living a life of grace which is a life of compassion? Are we acknowledging that we are recipients of an enormous, magnificent grace of God, and are we trying to live as redistributors of that grace? That's what I care about. Are we living grace? Are we aware that God is very much a part of all that comes to us that is good?

II. Woe to You Spirituality of Grace and Compassion

Several years ago, I shared an illustration in a Thanksgiving message. I had come in one Saturday morning from bow hunting, and I was not quite ready to go to the house. There's a cove behind my house. It's a pond, but it's actually a cove where the lake has brought in sand and dammed off that part. Many creatures live back there. There are two that I love to watch, and they are Mr. & Mrs. Beaver. I went to the pond on this particular Saturday. I was dressed in full camouflage. I eased back and was seated next to a tree hoping they might show themselves. I was enjoying the quietness of the moment before I went back to the house. I saw movement to my right and eased my eyes in that direction before I slowly turned my head and I saw a lanky body moving through the bushes. I recognized it as the rear end of a cat. As I looked closer it was part Siamese. I could tell from the way it moved and the way it looked. It was a male cat, so I named him Mr. Tom. I watched him move up on beyond the house and go to our dog food bowl to see if there were any scraps left. That was when Wateree Will was a small puppy. I caught them lying together in the sun a couple of times. But as soon as Mr. Tom saw me, he would take off. I started putting out food at night after we took our dog in the house. I'd get a glimpse of Mr. Tom as he would come by and eat the food and walk by the big window. Anytime I stepped out, Tom would be gone in a flash. I mean, he just didn't run off a little ways. He would leave. But he would slip in under the darkness of night and eat my food, enjoy my benevolence, partake of my grace without ever pausing long enough to acknowledge a thanksgiving or to acknowledge the source of this food. He had been living in the fear that if he paused long enough, I would take away his freedom.

I feed Mr. Tom every night. It's been almost three years now. I'd like to take him over to Dr. Denton, the veterinarian, and have him defleaed, deticked and dewormed and washed and cleaned up. I'd have him checked out to make sure he is physically fine. I wouldn't declaw him and put him in the house. I don't want to take away his freedom. I'd just like to make life a little better for him. That's all. I'd just like to show him a little grace.

God is that way with us. God has demonstrated to us an enormous amount of grace. Listen to the grace in this passage. Jesus says near the close of the 23rd chapter of Matthew, verse 37, "O Jerusalem, Jerusalem, you that killest the prophets and stonest them which are sent unto you, how I would have gathered you under my wing as a hen doth gather her chicks. But you wouldn't let me." You would not let me grace you in that fashion. God is the God of grace and it's unearned, it's free; but not free to God.

Have you seen the movie *The Last Emperor*? It is a movie of a child emperor of China, the last emperor of China. It's a child. This child is lavished with all of the luxury that being an emperor could bring to him. His brother says to him one day, "What happens when you are disobedient?

He said, "Someone else is punished."

Wow! Do you realize how theological that is? What happens when we are disobedient? Jesus Christ was punished. Grace is not free. Grace cost God God's life in a horrible crucifixion. That's how much God loves you. God loves you so much God desires to grace you and for you to live out that grace.

Conclusion

The *Boston Globe* reported this story in 1990. An engaged couple goes down to the Hyatt hotel in downtown Boston. They are making their wedding plans and they wanted to have their wedding reception at the Hyatt. They go through all the flowers that are going to be there and they pick the menu. They do all that stuff. The bill comes to $13,000. Half of the cost has to be put on deposit, so the bride writes a personal check for $6,500 of her money. She has done well, although she did not start well. She started out in a rescue mission, but she's educated herself, she's done well, and she's made good money. She writes the check and leaves it as a deposit. They go about making their wedding plans. Three days after the wedding invitations are sent out, the groom-to-be comes to her and says, "I don't think I can do this." So, he backs out. Of course, she is in a dilemma. She tries to recoup what she can and rearrange. You know about the plans of mice and men. In this case, it's mice and women. She goes down to the Hyatt and tells them what happened and the manager was just as empathic as she could be. She said, "Darling, this is not the first time this has happened. It has happened to people before. You'll get over it, you'll work through it. But I've got some sad news. The contract is a contract and you can only get $1,300 of your money back. That's all."

Wow! The deposit was $6,500, and she can only get $1,300 of it back. In jest, the manager says to her that she could have a banquet anyway and not lose any of her money.

She goes home distraught. She does not take the $1,300. After a little while, she goes back down to the Hyatt and says, "Let's plan a banquet. I want to keep that reservation. I want to change the menu, though. In honor of my ex-fiancé, we're going to have boneless chicken."

So they changed the menu to chicken cordon bleu. She sends out invitations to the rescue centers of the town, to the community missions of the town, to the bridges and the underpasses. She invites the transients—the street folks. Does this sound typical to you? She invites all these people to come to the Hyatt and enjoy this banquet. People come rolling Winn-Dixie buggies with all their belongings in it, people come from the rescue centers, from the bridges and the overpasses to the downtown Hyatt. And there in their disarray, they are served by waiters in tuxedos chicken cordon bleu, champagne, the finest Boston has to offer. I submit to you, that is grace. Grace redistributed through this jilted bride. She could have taken all that money and in many ways made life miserable for him. I have to watch myself, because when I read the story I start thinking of ways!

We are people who have been awesomely graced. Grace is compassion. Compassion is expressed to other people, our planet, and our universe. God help us to be people of grace.

Prayer: O Lord, we thank you even for religion because we know not all of it is graceless. Not all of it lives out its life in ungrace. Much of it does. We ask for even yet prophets who will stir it up, rekindle it, redeem it. But God, in the midst of it all, help us to be aware of what you want from us, which is to live a life of grace which is compassion—to be grace at home with our spouses, with our children, with our stepchildren, ex-spouses, at work, at play. Help us to be grace. In Jesus' name. Amen.

Let us share our benediction together, which is from the 5th chapter of I Peter, verse 10: "And the God of all grace, who called you to his eternal glory in Christ after you have suffered a little while, will himself restore you and make you strong, firm, and steadfast. To Him be the power forever and ever. Amen."

God bless you. May you be kept in His grace and mercy and be continually used as instruments of God's grace.

Chapter Twelve

Grace! It's Superfluous

TEXT:Romans 5:1–2; 12–15; 20–21

CIT: Paul said where sin abounded, grace did much more abound.

THESIS: Where sin abounds, grace is superfluous.

PURPOSE:*Major objective:* doctrinal

Specific objective: Through the power of the Holy Spirit, I hope to lead each of us in responding to the grace of God.

TITLE: "GRACE! IT'S SUPERFLUOUS"

INTRODUCTION

OUTLINE:

I.Standing in Grace Brings Justification—v. 1a

II.Standing in Grace Brings Peace and Joy—v. 1b

CONCLUSION

Dr. Eugene C. Rollins

Scripture Reading: Romans 5:1–2; 12 –15; 20–21

Therefore, since we have been justified through faith, we have peace with God through our Lord Jesus Christ, through whom we have gained access by faith into this grace in which we now stand. And we rejoice in the hope of the glory of God.

Therefore, just as sin entered the world through one man, and death through sin, and in this way death came to all men, because all sinned— for before the law was given, sin was in the world. But sin is not taken into account when there is no law. Nevertheless, death reigned from the time of Adam to the time of Moses, even over those who did not sin by breaking a command, as did Adam, who was a pattern of the one to come.

But the gift is not like the trespass. For if the many died by the trespass of the one man, how much more did God's grace and the gift that came by the grace of the one man, Jesus Christ, overflow to the many?

The law was added so that the trespass might increase. But where sin increased, grace increased all the more, so that, just as sin reigned in death, so also grace might reign through righteousness to bring eternal life through Jesus Christ our Lord.

Introduction

Someone said this morning that I was going to need to define the word used in my sermon title. Well, I have done that already. Look on the bulletin cover. The word "sheer" means pure and unmixed. Grace is the pure and unmixed, undeserved, unearned, unmerited, incredible kindness of God. That's superfluous. Let's look in this text and see if we can find a grace that is like that. I'd love to have time to read the whole 5th chapter of Romans, but I have just included the parts that talk about grace being abundant and abounding. The word of the Lord.

I. Standing in Grace Brings Justification

The text is saying where sin abounds, grace over-abounds. Grace is much more, no matter what the sin. The beautiful phrase in this text is: "We are now justified having access to the grace in which we now stand." So if you can get the picture of standing in or standing under an umbrella of grace. Let's see what this grace does. I love that old hymn "Standing on the Promises." You know if you keep standing on the promises and standing in the promises, sooner or later you will be sitting on the premises. If you keep standing in grace, standing under grace, you will sooner or later be in the presence of pure grace in the premises and in the presence of God Almighty in our eternal home. So let's look at this text and see what standing in or standing under grace means.

It says first of all that it means being justified. I do not have the words— I am not verbally adequate this morning to describe to you what that word means in its entirety. There are many words in the Scriptures that try to get at this idea. Forgiveness is one of those words. The Scripture tells us that God forgives us. The word "forgive" in its Greek origin means to let go of, to release the wish, the desire to get even or to harm or to hurt. So when God says in God's word that "God in Christ forgives us," then God has released the wish, the desire, turned loose of the wish and desire, to hurt us or to get even with us for our sin. Now that is a meaningful concept, but it is not as beautiful as justification.

The Scripture also talks about us being pardoned. That God pardons us. Well, one who is convicted of sin, a crime, and is institutionalized, can often be pardoned. Now that does not say that he is innocent. It says that he is guilty, but for whatever reason, he has been pardoned. That too is a meaningful concept. We are guilty, and the Scriptures tell us that God did pardon us, so God forgave us, let go of the wish to harm us for our sin. Pardoned us, released us from the shackles and the enslavement of sin.

The scripture uses another meaningful word in that it is called reconciliation. God has reconciled us. You have a party over here and a party over here, and they are torn down the middle through some kind of schism. God has taken those two parties, meaning us and God, and brought them together in a reconciliation. That too is a meaningful word, but none of them hold a candle to the word "justification."

Paul says over and over again that we have been justified before God. I want to tell you simply what that means. It means that God forgave us. Yes. It means that God pardoned us. Yes. It means that God reconciled us. Yes. But, it also means that God looks at us through the eyes of God's son, who came and lived and died for us. God looks at us through his eyes and what God sees is us just as if we never sinned. That is what justification means. It means to be seen just as if you've never sinned. Now let me see if I can illustrate this.

In the days of the Russian terror, Joseph Stalin was reputed to have had a psychologist that worked with him who was world renowned for getting a confession out of a person whether or not the person had committed the crime. Committing a crime or not was immaterial. This psychologist was so good, he could get a confession out of a person who would serve time for a crime maybe he or she did not commit. There came an interviewer from the West who interviewed the psychologist. He asked him what his secret was. What was the key to his success in gaining all those confessions from people? The psychologist said, "I operate on the Mongolian peasant hypothesis."

The interviewer looked at him kind of funny and said, "What in the world does that mean?"

"I believe that every person has a Mongolian peasant within them."

"You are going to have to explain."

The psychologist explains. A nobody person is ushered into this magnificent business office with these beautiful oak walls, and all of the pictures of the government and everything else are on the walls. He is seated before this big mahogany desk and the desk is uncluttered with paper, and it has all these expensive pens on it. Behind the desk is a general, dressed sharply in his uniform with a whole chest full of ribbons and everything else. The general says to the person, as he pulls open one of the drawers of the big mahogany desk, "I have a million rubles in this drawer. Look at it. For you. It's yours."

The person says, "What do I have to do?"

He says, "You see this red button on the desk? All you have to do is hit this red button, and if you hit this red button, these million rubles are yours."

The person says, "What happens when I hit that red button?"

"A Mongolian peasant dies."

"What did he do?" asked the person.

"He didn't do anything. That's immaterial. It doesn't matter. Just a Mongolian peasant dies when you hit this red button, and when you hit this red button, you get a million rubles. That's all you've got to do."

So the guy sits there for a moment, reaches over and hits the red button, and the general gives him his million rubles and he leaves. Five years later, he commits suicide, living in the same little house that he lived in five years earlier, and there is a sack under his bed containing a million rubles. The psychologist said, "I believe that in every person's life, there is a Mongolian peasant, and all I have to do is find it and pick at it, and pick at it, and pick at it, until that person will confess to anything, ANYTHING to get freed from the guilt and the shame of that Mongolian peasant."[16]

That is another way of saying what the Bible says. The Scripture says that all of us have sinned. There is our Mongolian peasant. All of us. The way I get at it, sometimes when I feel shame, a deep sense of shame and guilt, within a client, I'll say to the client, "It's 11:00 on Sunday night. There is a knock at your door. You go to the door and the door is opened. This person calls your name and says to you, 'The world now knows the truth about you.' " I pause and let it hang in the air for a second or two, and then I'll say, "John, what is that truth? What is that Mongolian peasant that haunts you, that disturbs your sleep? What is that which causes you to act in ways that you do not want to act? What is it? What is it?"

II. Standing in Grace Brings Peace

I've read on several accounts where forty, forty-five year old persons, primarily men, have sent back to their alma mater, their universities, their degrees with a letter of explanation saying they had cheated all the way through college and that they do not deserve the degree. I've wondered how that Mongolian peasant has haunted them all these years to the point where they could take it no longer. They could live with it no longer, and they send back the degree.

There is within all of us a Mongolian peasant. There is within all of us sin, shortcomings, mistakes. There is within all of us shame and guilt and at times grief and at times depression about that. Hear the word of grace. God says as you stand in and under this word of grace, "I see you just as if you've never sinned. It's not that you're forgiven, not that you're pardoned. I see you just as if it never happened." WOW! That's grace. That is standing in grace and standing under grace, and in that standing brings us justification, just as if we've never sinned. And that justification brings us peace. A peace that the Scripture says passes all human understanding.

A young man was creating a list of what he wanted to attain as he entered his vocational life. He had on that list wealth, vocational reputation, and fame. He had 8–10 items on that list. An elderly man was looking at the list and said to him, "You've left out something."

The young man looked at him and said, "What?"

"You've left out an ingredient that will cause all these others to be meaningless, and that is peace of mind."

In Lieberman's classic, *Peace of Mind,* he tells us that we learn in the book of Joshua that there is no peace without a deep sense of justification. There is no peace without a sense of I'm standing in and under God's grace, God's unmerited, undeserved, unearned kindness toward me. Without that, there is no peace. There is no social peace without soul peace. There is no soul peace without a harmonious relationship to our Creator. Soul peace. Soul peace is found in that stand of grace. Standing under the justification of God, as I am aware that God looks at me and sees me just as if I have never sinned. Not that I am forgiven,

I am. Not that I am pardoned, I am. Not that I am reconciled, I am. But, just as if it never happened. That is what is abundant. Standing in that grace brings the justification. The justification brings an abiding inner peace, and that abiding inner peace brings joy. Not happiness. I'm not much on happiness. You can find happiness anywhere, absolutely anywhere. You can find it in a bottle. You can find it in a pill. You can find happiness anywhere and almost everywhere, but joy—that is something that is deep within that is contented. That's something deep within that is OK. That comes out of peace. Peace comes out of justification. Justification comes out of our stance and grace.

Several years ago, a man came to me and started sharing his divorce. He was so embittered, crying, and then became angry at his wife for leaving him. That anger spilled over to the church because his church would not allow him to partake of communion because he was divorced. His church had been very meaningful to him, and now he was blocked out of the church because she had left him and he was divorced. We talked on for a little bit and I asked when his divorce was finalized. He thought and gave me a date of 15 years ago. Fifteen years ago, and he was handling it, grieving over it, anxious about it, angry about it, as if it took place last week. When you are standing in that fashion, without joy, without peace, to be able to know that I can change that stance to a stance of grace where God looks at me just as if I've never sinned; therefore, I can look at this face in the mirror, look at this face every morning when I shave and say, "You're OK."

Yes, there is more than one Mongolian peasant back there. But God doesn't see it. You stand in grace, and you are justified by that stand in grace. It is that justification that cleans up a life, straightens up a life, makes us livable with ourselves and livable with others.

One of our members passed this old poem to me a couple of weeks ago—one that I'd read many years ago, but I'd forgotten. I believe it has been put into a song. This is what it says:

" 'Twas battered and scarred and the auctioneer thought that is scarcely worth his while to waste much time on the old violin, but he held it up with a smile.

"What am I bidding good folks he cried. Who will start the bidding for me?

A dollar, a dollar, now who will make it two? Two dollars, now who will make it three? Three dollars once, three dollars twice, going for three bucks."

"No!" From the room far back, a gray haired man came forward and picked up the bow. Wiping the dust from the old violin and tightening the loose strings, he played a melody pure and sweet, as a caroling angel sings. The music ceased, and the auctioneer's little voice that was quiet and low said,

"What am I bidding for the old violin?" and he held it up with the bow.

"A thousand dollars, who'll make it three? Three thousand once, three thousand twice. Going, going, gone," he said. People cheered, but some of them cried, "We do not quite understand what changed its worth?" Swift came the reply, "The touch of the master's hand." Many a man with life out of tune, battered and torn by sin is auctioned cheap to a faultless crowd, much like the old violin. A mess of pottage, a glass of wine, a game and he travels on. He's going once, he's going twice, he's going and he's almost gone, but the master comes, and the foolish crowd never can quite understand the worth of a soul and the change that's wrought by the touch of the master's hand."

That is grace.

Prayer: Oh, Lord, if we're honest this morning, every one of us has a Mongolian peasant inside. Every one of us, in the quietness of the night, when we are alone with ourselves, the shadow comes out of the closet. The shameful condemning voice rehearses the past. Help us to know experientially that when these times come, we can look deeper within and say, Standing in grace I am justified. God sees me just as if I have never sinned. Give us the peace and the joy out of that knowledge. May it be so, in Jesus' name. Amen.

I want our benediction to be our bulletin cover, and I want you to add two words at the end: "to me." Alright, let's share it together: Grace is the sheer undeserved, unearned, unmerited, incredible kindness of God to me. God bless you, and may God keep you in grace until we meet again. God bless you, and thank you for coming.

❧ *Chapter Thirteen* ❧

Grace! It's Overcoming

TEXT:Romans 5:1–11

CIT: Paul said that standing in grace gives us a spirit that can overcome the world.

THESIS: Standing in grace, we can actively overcome and conquer the trials and tribulations of life.

PURPOSE: *Major objective:* doctrinal

Specific objective: Through the power of the Holy Spirit, I hope to lead each of us in appropriating the grace of God for our lives.

TITLE: "GRACE! IT'S OVERCOMING"

INTRODUCTION

OUTLINE:

I.In Grace We Rejoice—vv. 2–3

II.In Grace Our Sufferings Produce Perseverance—v. 3

III.In Grace Our Perseverance Produces Character—v. 4

IV.In Grace Our Character Produces Hope—v. 4

V.In Grace Our Hope Is Overcoming —vv. 4-5

CONCLUSION

Scripture Reading: Romans 5:1–11

Therefore since we have been justified through faith, we have peace with God, through our Lord Jesus Christ through whom we've gained access by faith into this grace in which we now stand. And we rejoice in the hope of the glory of God, not only so, but we also rejoice in our sufferings because we know that suffering produces perseverance; perseverance, character; and character, hope; and hope does not disappoint us because God has poured out His love into our hearts by the Holy Spirit, whom He's given us. You see, at just the right time, when we were still powerless, Christ died for the ungodly. Very rarely will anyone die for a righteous man, though for a good man, someone might dare to die, but God demonstrates His own love for us in this. While we were still sinners, Christ died for us. Since we have now been justified by His blood, how much more shall we be saved from God's wrath through Him. For if we were God's enemies, we were reconciled to Him through the death of His son. How much more having been reconciled shall we be saved through His life. Not only is this so, but we also rejoice in God through our Lord Jesus Christ, through whom we have now received reconciliation.

Introduction

Back in the late 1960s, there was a book by Dr. Harris that formed the foundation for the movement called Transactual Analysis. There was a time in my early therapeutic upbringing that Transactual Analysis was the real fad going in therapy circles. Now it has died out. I have a friend who said, "That's the story of my life. Just about the time I get certified in a school, it peters out." But Dr. Harris wrote a book entitled *I'm Okay, You're Okay,* and it spread across this nation. The problem with that, I think part of the problem with Transactual Analysis, is that there is a deep, deep part of us that knows I'm not OK. I can say it a thousand times a day. I can get up and go to the mirror and do what some of the pop psychologists say, "Talk to yourself. Tell yourself how wonderful you are. Look in the mirror and tell yourself what marvelous traits you have and what wonderful attributes fill your life." I can do that a thousand times a day, but there is still a part of me that knows deep down, there is a part that is simply not OK. I don't know where ALL that comes from, but I know where some of it comes from.

I. In Grace We Rejoice

I was talking to a fellow yesterday, and since dove season is upon us, we were talking about that. He said to me that he is always invited to a grand, wonderful dove shoot, but they have it on a Sunday afternoon and he never goes. And I said quickly, "Well, if you took your preacher with you, you wouldn't feel that way." I tried to talk with him about it saying, "Surely you're mature enough to know God doesn't have a problem with you dove hunting on Sunday afternoon," but before I could get there, he said to me, "Every time I think about going, I see my papa standing there with that stick." Ah ha! So that's where it comes from. You know a lot of our theology; in fact, most of our theology, came through Mama anyway, or Daddy, with that stick. But most of us, especially in the South, have been schooled in those more conservative fundamental churches where we are taught very, very clearly that we are being watched, and God is writing down what God sees in a book.

It is like the seventh chapter of Job, where Job in his suffering cries out to God, "Will you not take your eyes OFF of me long enough for me to swallow my spit?" You know we talk about Job being patient. Job wasn't patient. You need to re-read that book. Job was not patient at ALL. He cried out a lot, "God, why are you doing this to me? Why are you allowing this to happen? Where are you?" But a lot of those teachings and a lot of those feelings came to us intuitively. Others were very obviously placed upon us. But ALL of that we carry with us and there are times that we just know deep within us, I'm not OK. I can say, "I'm OK, you're OK, and we're OK." I can do that on and on, but it still comes down to the bottom line, I'm not OK. So hear this: God's grace is this, you're not OK, and that's OK. Through justification we have been ushered into the grace in which we now stand. I love that phrase in our test. We have access into the grace in which we now stand, and the grace in which we now stand says to us that God sees us just as if we've never sinned. That is grace. You can't talk me out of my sin. I know I've sinned. If God knows my faults, you can't talk me into the fact that I have no vile thoughts. I know I do. But God looks at me through the eyes of justification and through the eyes of justification, God sees me just as if I've never sinned. That is justification. And it is because of justification that we have reason to rejoice.

II. In Grace Our Sufferings Produce Perseverance

And then the text takes it a little deeper. Not only can we rejoice in the fact that I'm not OK and God says, "That's OK," but we can rejoice in our sufferings. Now that starts bringing something else into it. How is it, God, that we can rejoice in our sufferings? How is it that when hard times come, when trials and tribulations come, when our dreams and our hopes fall around us like cut grass, how is it that we can rejoice? God says in the word, "Rejoice in this." Those trials and tribulations are going to produce in you "hupomeno." What in the world is that, preacher? Well, it is translated here, perseverance. It is translated in other translations, endurance, but not any of those English translations get to the real meaning of that Greek word "hupomeno." The word "hupomeno" means to stand up under pressure, but it means more than that. That is a kind of passive stance. Hupomeno is an active stance. An active stance under suffering that produces a character that we will talk about in just a moment.

Hupomeno is like this: it is when Beethoven heard that he was going deaf and there was not anything that could be done. Can you imagine— the verdict of that to a musician, that he is going deaf? Here is what he said, in the midst of that trial and tribulation, Beethoven said, "I'll take life by the throat." Now that's hupomeno. That is not passively yielding ourselves to whatever trial and whatever tribulation is upon us and just passively enduring it. Hupomeno is actively standing in the context of the pressure that is upon us.

Sir Walter Scott was bankrupt, not because of anything that he did, but because his publishers went bankrupt. Sir Walter Scott said, "No one will ever look at me and say 'the poor fellow.' I will pay off the debts with my own hands." That is hupomeno. That is being unwilling to lay down and let trials and circumstances, trials and tribulations make a victim out of us. God says that when these kind of trials and when these kind of tribulations come, if we will stand in grace. . . "into this grace in which we stand," if we'll stand under God's justifying grace, the trials and tribulations that come to us will serve to produce hupomeno and endurance that is active in us. An active endurance. I may not be preaching to anyone but myself this morning, but I'm in a spot where I need that. I need to know that the trials and tribulations of the day are not going to be my ruin, but they are going to be the ingredient that God uses to bring about a greater since of stick-to-itiveness. Not all philosophers believe what this word is saying. The Scripture says we can rejoice in our sufferings because the first result of that rejoicing as we are standing in grace is that we are going to be empowered to endure actively. Not passively, but actively endure. One philosopher, I forget his name right now, but the book was around 1900, he said, "Suffering does not ignoble the character. Suffering most often makes us petty and vindictive," and there is some truth in that, if we allow it to. Suffering can make us pessimistic. Suffering can make us petty. Suffering can make us vindictive. Life gives us testimony to that, but life also gives us testimony to the fact that when we stand in grace, yield ourselves to God, and even yield ourselves to the trials and tribulations that are taking place, in the spirit, in the grace, ask God to use this to hupomeno us, cause us to stand actively persevering.

III. In Grace Our Perseverance Produces Character

And then the Scripture says perseverance produces character. "Dorime," the Greek word here, is the word that gives rise to the process that we take gold and sterling silver through. Gold has to be burned in the fire to rid itself of the impurities. Silver, the same way. Silver has to undergo the trial and the test of fire to rid itself of its impurities. The Scripture is telling us that as we stand in God's grace when trials and tribulations come, God will use it to rid our lives of the impurities and cause us to come out of that with a character that we could not have otherwise come out with.

Two weavers of old, Ivan and John, were both new to this weave shop. I understand that story a little more fully now, since I've seen in Ireland the weave shops that are still operated by hand. This was one of those shops where the weaving was done by hand, as the weaver moved that shuttle back and forth himself. As the day started, both were brought just a small amount of bright golden cloth. Ivan thought it was such a little amount, "I will not even use it."

John picked it up and used it. A little later, there was some dark cloth brought in.

Ivan says, "There is too much of that. I can't use all that," so he only used part of it. John used it all. There were darker shades of purple, and again Ivan said, "No, that's too dark. I'm not going to use it all," and John used it all. Then some lighter colors of orange came and Ivan said, "That's too little to use. I'll not even put it in," and John used it all.

At the end of the day, when the master weaver came by, Ivan said to him, "Your cloth, your cloth, it's all wrong. I didn't get enough of this. I got too much of that. I really had a problem with your cloth." He looks at John's weaving and there in the context of all of the darkness of the purples and the dark threads, there are those golden threads and those orange threads that bring it out.

Hear me now. It is not what we're given that creates the pattern. It is what we do with it that creates the pattern. It is not what happens to us that is important. It is what happens to what happens to us. It is not the thread that life dumps on us. It is how we weave the thread into the overall being of who we are. If we want to let those dark purples and those dark blacks cause us to be petty and vindictive, then we will . . . mean spirited, then we will . . . pessimistic, then we will. But if standing in God's grace, we want to be seen as justified, and we want God to take these threads of trials and tribulations and allow us to weave them into our lives in such a way that it will produce character, then we will. A character that has been tested in the fire, a character that has come through the tribulations and the trial and has stood the test, that kind of character is imbued with hope.

IV. In Grace Our Character Produces Hope

Remember the passage starts out with hope. Not only does this justification give us peace, it gives us hope. Not only can we rejoice, but we can rejoice in our suffering. We can rejoice through our suffering because the result gives us a hope; and in grace, that hope is overcoming.

That hope can help us to be overcomers through our trials and our tribulations.

Conclusion

I received this last week through one of our members. Several of my members often send me these little e-mail things, and if you get those little e-mail stories, you need to consider, on the one hand if the story looks totally impossible to be historical, it probably is. It's probably not historical, but that's really not the point. If there is no historical truth, there may be much mythological truth. What is the value of the story? What is the story trying to teach? Back years ago they dug wells by hand. Some of you are old enough to realize that. They didn't have these little drilled holes in the ground about 12 inches. They had a huge hole, where men got down in that hole with picks and shovels and buckets and pulleys, and they dug the well and hoisted the dirt out. They dug and dug until they hit water. Well, this old farmer had a well like that, which had long since produced water, and he had not had a chance to cover it up. His donkey fell into the hole. He heard the donkey braying, and he went and looked down into the well. He realized that his old donkey had fallen into the well and now he was wondering what in the world was he going to do. He started thinking, well, the old donkey was pretty old, and I was going to have to put him down pretty soon anyway. I need to cover the hole up, so I will call in some friends, and we will just do two things at once. We will just bury the old donkey and cover up this old well that needed to be covered. So he calls in a lot of friends and they come in and move some dirt. There they are with their shovels, standing around that old well, talking and having fellowship with each other and they start throwing in dirt. As they throw in dirt, they hear the old donkey bray and they say, "Well, he's going to quit in a minute." Sure enough, he quit in a minute. They continued to throw dirt in the well and fellowship with each other. After a little while, the old farmer looked down into the well, and lo and behold, the donkey was halfway up the well. He watched as a shovel of dirt was thrown in and landed on the old donkey's back. He shook it off and took another step up. So after a little while, the donkey just stepped over that little foot ledge and walked out of the well. Now, did that really happen? I don't care if that really happened or not. Here is the truth! When life throws a shovelful on you, shuck it off and take another step. Shuck it off and take another step. The truth is, life will bury you whether you're ready of not, if you'll let it. And a lot of people, standing around with a lot of shovels, will cover you up. Shuck it off and take another step. That is hupomeno. That is standing in God's grace, knowing deep within, I'm not OK, and that is OK.

Prayer: Oh, Lord, thank you that you are so honest in your revealed word, that life is not always grand, glorious, and wonderful, that in life, dirt does fall upon us. There are attempts to cover us up. Life does seek to get us down. Trial, tribulation, and suffering is part of our life's lot, but in the midst of it all, Lord you tell us, to stand in your grace, and your grace will produce in us overcomers. Help us to believe it. Amen.

❧ Chapter Fourteen ❧

Grace! It's Sharing

TEXT:Matthew 18:21–35

CIT: Jesus told a parable of a servant who was graced with forgiveness; and with the grace, he was expected to grace others with the grace of forgiveness.

THESIS: We are graced by God to be grace to others.

PURPOSE: *Major objective:* doctrinal

Specific objective: Through the power of the Holy Spirit, I hope to lead each of us in sharing the grace we have been given.

TITLE: "GRACE! IT'S SHARING"

INTRODUCTION

OUTLINE:

I. The Master's Grace—vv. 21–27

II. The Servant's Ungrace—vv. 28–31

III. The Master's Ungrace—vv. 32–34

IV. We Are Graced to Be Graced—v. 35

CONCLUSION

Scripture Reading: Matthew 18:21–35

Then Peter came to Jesus and asked, "Lord, how many times shall I forgive my brother when he sins against me? Up to seven times?" Jesus answered, "I tell you, not seven times, but seventy seven times." Therefore the kingdom of heaven is like a king who went to settle accounts with his servants. As he began the settlement, a man who owed him 10,000 talents was brought to him. Since he was not able to pay, the master ordered that he and his wife and his children and all that he had be sold to repay the debt. The servant fell on his knees before him. "Be patient with me," he begged, "and I will pay back everything." The servant's master took pity on him, "Cancel the debt and let him go." When the servant went out, he found one of his fellow servants who owed him 100 denary. He grabbed him and began to choke him. "Pay back what you owe me," he demanded. His fellow servant fell to his knees and begged him, "Be patient with me, I will pay you back." But he refused. Instead he went off and had the man thrown into prison until he could pay the debt. When the other servants saw what had happened, they were greatly distressed and went and told their master everything that had happened. Then the master called the servant. "You wicked servant," he said. "I canceled all that debt of yours because you begged me to. Shouldn't you have had mercy on your fellow servant, just as I had on you?" In anger, his master turned him over to the jailers until he should pay back all he owed. This is how my heavenly father will treat each of you, unless you forgive your brother from your heart.

Introduction

This sermon is a cornerstone, a rudimentary foundation to the entire "Grace" series. We do not have ears to hear oftentimes. In Revelation, it is said over and over again the prayer that we would have ears to hear. One of the reasons that we do not have ears to hear the message of grace is because of this message. It is because of the context of this, Jesus' parable. It is because of this that grace is resisted. It is because of this that we have become so ritualistic in our churches and graceless in our churches. It is because of this that we will not have ears to hear. But it is not just this parable, it is all over. In Matthew 5:9, just as those beautiful beatitudes start, the word says, "Blessed are the merciful, for they shall obtain mercy." Mercy and grace. "Blessed are the graceful, because they shall be graced." We will not look at the underbelly of that. We will not hear the other side of that: "Cursed are the merciless, for they shall be damned." That's exactly what it is saying, but we will not let it say that. We will not hear it say that. It is in that beautiful beatitude section where Matthew records the Lord's Prayer. There is only one portion of the Lord's Prayer that is illustrated, that is augmented, that is talked about, and that one line in the model prayer is, "Forgive others as you have been forgiven." That is the only portion of the prayer that is talked about. Why? Because it's the absolute most difficult part of the prayer to do. We will not hear the fullness of grace because of what grace demands of us.

I. The Master's Grace

Peter comes to Jesus to talk about forgiveness. Jesus has been talking about forgiveness in this text. Peter says to the Lord, "How many times do we have to do this? Do we have to keep on forgiving and forgiving, seven times?" Now, Peter knew full well that the Greek symbolic meaning of the number seven was "full and complete." He was asking Jesus, Must we just go on and on forgiving? Jesus, playing his game, his semantic game, his numerology game, says, "Yes, seventy times seven." Then Jesus said this, "The kingdom of God, the kingdom of heaven is likened unto."

You know any time we're reading the New Testament and we are reading along devotionally studying and we come across a passage which says "and the kingdom of God is likened unto this," something within us should say, whoops, flag time. Important issue here! Crucial issue here! What's Jesus saying? "The kingdom of God is likened unto." Beware! Listen! Ears perk up like a German shepherd's. What is to be said? Jesus said there is a master who assesses that it is time to settle up. So he calls his servants in and he is settling up with them, with what they owe him. One servant comes in, and . . . I'm going to make these numbers contemporary because you do not have any idea what talents mean, and you do not have any idea what denary mean. I'm going to use the common expression of what these terms would be equal today in dollar value. The master calls this servant up and says, you owe me twelve million dollars—1,000 talents—pay up. And he said, I can't do it right now. If you'll give me a little grace or give me a little mercy here, if you'll give me a little time, I'll pay you back. He falls on his knees before the master and he pleads his case and says, I'll pay it all back if you'll just give me a little time. I'll pay it back. He may have given him reasons why he was unable to pay him and why he was so much in debt. The master is moved. He says to him, Alright, I'm going to give you thirty more days. No, I'm going to give you another year. No, he says to the servant, your debt is cancelled. Twelve million dollars— boom! You are forgiven. Your debt is cancelled. Can you imagine how that servant left?

II. The Servant's Ungrace

It becomes complicated here because the servant leaves and goes to another servant who owes him money. He grabs him by the neck and he says, Pay me back the $17.00 that you owe me. The servant says I don't have it. I can't pay you back right now. The first servant says, Tough! You owe it to me, and he puts him in jail. Well, the rumor mill always works, always has. The rumor mill was very busy about the master who cancelled his servant's twelve million dollar debt. Can you imagine how the rumor mill worked? It always works more on the negative side. Can you imagine how it really worked when this servant who was given twelve million dollars goes to the next servant under him and chokes him and throws him in jail for a seventeen dollar debt? Oh, I can imagine. This rumor mill makes its way to the master and the master says, "What? The servant I forgave and cancelled twelve million dollars put someone else in jail for a debt of seventeen dollars? Are you kidding? Get him back in here."

So they bring the servant back in. And he says, "What have you done? What are you doing? I forgave you twelve million dollars and you go choke, threaten, and put this man in jail for a seventeen dollar debt. I cancel what I cancelled. You still owe me twelve million dollars. Throw him in jail." And they put him in jail.

III. The Master's Ungrace

Now let me pause to say here that as a Southern Baptist years ago, they did not own my soul, and I . . . because I was not a systematic theologian . . . did not have to systematize and explain how they can believe in "once saved, always saved" with this kind of text. In all these years as a Presbyterian whose soul is still not owned by a denomination, I do not systematically try to explain away how we are elected to salvation and our election is sure with these kinds of text. I just preach the text, and the text says there was a servant who was graced and the servant would not live out his grace. His grace was cancelled and he was thrown in jail. For those who can sit back on their laurels and say, "once saved, always saved," I'm as happy as a bug in a rug. For those on the other hand that can say, "Well, I'm elected and my election is sure," I kind of sit with the Methodists who say, "you best persevere." This text says you are graced to be grace. You have been forgiven that you might live out your forgiveness, and if you are unwilling to live out your forgiveness, you should question your forgiveness. You have just burned the bridge that you yourself must cross. Always. That's why we don't like grace. Oh, I'd much rather, in response to being graced, I'd much rather be absolutely faithful in the worship of the Lord and put my money in that basket and in that plate. Oh, yes! Put my money in there, and come and sing my hymns and sing in the choir and preach and hear good sermons and listen attentively, and listen to the prayers. I'd rather do all of that . . . ritualistically, rather than to have to go out that door saying, "I've been forgiven. I now must live forgivingly. I've been graced, and in being graced, I'm obligated to be grace. That's all I'm obligated to do. That's all I'm obligated to be. . . is to be grace."

Forgiven to be forgiving. Graced to be grace. This servant was unwilling to do that and the master called him back in.

IV. We Are Graced to Be Grace

Mary Par talks in her book about an uncle in Texas who had a conflict with his wife about her overexpenditure of money on sugar. They get in this conflict and into a battle. She goes into her room and slams the door. He goes into his room and slams the door. He waits on her to come into his room, and she waits on him to come into her room. They have this Mexican standoff for years. Finally, he says, "This is enough," and he calls in a moving company. He takes a saw and saws the house right down the middle. He gets the moving company, and they move his half of the house on the other side of the trees. For the next forty years, they each live in half a house, never speaking again to each other. They never realized they had been graced to be grace. And when we refuse to be grace, our own grace must be questioned. Must be questioned. We must question it.

This past Friday night, Linda and I were having dinner out on the deck with candles, enjoying the sun setting out over the lake. I had fixed us a steak and just as we started eating, she said, "You overcooked my steak. You always overcook my steak."

I said, "That's a contaminated statement. Last Friday night, you said it was the most perfect steak you've ever eaten." Tonight you're saying I always over cook 'em.

Well, that old mill hill redneck part of me imagined myself reaching over into her plate and getting her steak and throwing it to the dog and saying, "Enjoy!" Now, I didn't do that, you know. I do have more sense than to do that. But I thought of this text and I hope you can put yourself in the text. The text cried out to me, "Eugene, you have been forgiven twelve million dollars. You gotta forgive this seventeen. Always. Every time. I don't care what it's about or who it is."

Here's a family with two brothers who have not spoken for fifteen years because of a fight when Mama's will was read. You can't keep living that way. You've burned the bridge that you must cross. You're not being graceful. You're not forgiving. You can't continue that way. Don't count on once saved, always saved. Don't count on election to perfection. You are graced to be grace. That's what God asks of us. That's what we must be . . . embodiment of grace. Does it mean we let people run over us? No. But it means we must live in the context of forgiveness.

A Jewish rabbi kept putting off the beautiful opportunity of coming to America. Three times he turned it down, and finally when he came to America, he said, "I had to forgive Adolf Hitler. I could not bring him within myself to a new country. I'm graced by this new land. I could not bring ungrace into its presence."

We are graced. God's unmerited blessings are ours for one purpose . . . that we might be grace.

I love one of Victor Hugo's novels where he talks about Jean Valjean, a Frenchman who had a rugged life as a child and was notorious for his rages. After spending time in prison, he was released. In those days in France, a prisoner had to carry a card notating the fact that he was a prisoner, and Valjean could not get a rooming place to board because when asked for identification he had to show this card. No one would give him a room. So he slept out for four nights in the elements. Then he came to a bishop's house, and the bishop let him in. The bishop's sister fixed him a meal and gave him a bed. In the wee hours of the morning, while the bishop and his sister slept, Valjean got up and rummaged through the house and took all of the silver and put it in a pillowcase and left. As he was trying to dispose of it the next day, they recognized in the little town who the silver belonged to. Two policemen brought him back to the bishop's house. When the bishop opened the door and saw the policemen and Valjean, he said, "You forgot something, Valjean. You did not take the silver candlesticks."

The police looked at him and asked, "Did he not steal these?"

The bishop said, "No, no, no. They were given to him and he went off and forgot the silver candlesticks."

He goes in and gathers up the silver candlesticks, and he gives them to Valjean and puts them in the pillowcase. Then the police leave, and he says to Valjean, "You must use the proceeds of this silver to make an honest man of yourself," and he bids him farewell.

That's not the end of the story, for there is a detective that dedicates his life to proving that Jean Valjean was a thief. The detective follows him, and his own life is saved by Valjean. He is so deeply unwilling and unable to accept this thief's grace, he commits suicide. Graced to be graced, folks.[17]

Conclusion

On April 9, 1865, Robert E. Lee mounted Traveler, he thought, for the last time. This magnificent animal had taken him through so many battles and had been so faithful and so true. He rode into Appomattox leading his little tattered, torn group of surrendered soldiers, and there he met General Grant. Lee asked Grant, "What are the terms of the surrender?"

Grant said, "There are no terms. Tell your men to take their horses and their belongings and go back south to their little farms and start their lives over again. And you take Traveler and go back home." Lee, deeply moved, removed his sword and extended it to General Grant, and General Grant refused it. As long as General Robert E. Lee lived, no one could say anything negative about General Grant in his presence.

That is grace. That kind of grace we have been given, only much more so. Our sins have been forgiven. Yeah, we have been pardoned. Grace means we have been pardoned. Pardoned means we have been made in God's eyes as if we have never, ever sinned. Justified. What would it be like if we could truly believe that we were graced? Every night, we could place our heads on our pillows knowing that we are free from guilt, from shame, from mistakes. We are free . . . liberated. And what would it be like to get up the next morning and to look in the mirror, putting on our makeup or shaving our faces, saying, "I am free of guilt and shame. I am free to walk out my door and to share that kind of forgiveness and grace with everyone else"? What kind of world would it be? It would be a world of grace. A world where unhealthy shame is obsolete. A world where healthy shame has lost its steam. A world where we know we are of great worth when we accept the grace we do not deserve. A world where bad choices of the past do not determine our worth of today, nor forfeit our worth for tomorrow. A world where we dare to feel, when guilty we are, for we know our guilt can be forgiven. A world where we celebrate our imperfections. A world where we can feel silly without feeling shame. A world where grace gives us reason to be proud of ourselves. A world where the lightness of grace lifts the heaviness of shame. A world where joy is the whole point of life. Graced . . . to be grace.

Let us pray: Oh Jesus, why will we not have ears to hear? Why will we not open our hearts to be freed from our own dungeons of guilt and grief? Why will we not stand in the shower of that grace only to walk out soaked with it and sharing it with others? Help us. In Jesus' name. Amen.

Chapter Fifteen

Grace! It's Freedom

TEXT:Galatians 5:1–6

CIT: Paul warned the Galatian Christians that they could not put their confidence in a legal system while putting their trust in the grace of God.

THESIS: Our soul's freedom is in grace plus nothing.

PURPOSE: *Major objective:* doctrinal

Specific objective: Through the power of the Holy Spirit, I hope to lead each of us in trusting God's grace in Christ for our salvation.

TITLE: "GRACE! IT'S FREEDOM"

INTRODUCTION

OUTLINE:

I.Christ's Grace Is Freedom—v. 1

II.Religious Rule-Keeping Is Bondage—v. 1

III.Grace, Faith, and Love Are All That Count—v. 6

CONCLUSION

Scripture Reading: Galatians 5:1–6

It is for freedom that Christ has set us free. Stand firm, then, and do not let yourselves be burdened again by a yoke of slavery. Mark my words, I, Paul, tell you that if you let yourselves be circumcised, Christ will be of no value to you at all. Again, I declare to every man who lets himself be circumcised, that he is obligated to obey the whole law. You, trying to be justified by law, have been alienated from Christ. You have fallen away from grace, but by faith we eagerly await through the spirit of righteousness for which we hope. For in Christ Jesus, neither circumcised nor uncircumcision has any value. The only thing that counts is faith expressing itself through love.

Introduction

September 30th, the fifth Sunday of September at 8:00, I'll be preaching again at the Kershaw prison. I'll be using this text, and I'm going to say to those inmates that I am preaching about something this morning that everyone of you want, everyone of you without exception wants freedom. Then I'm going to say something like, there are those of you who will be released from here, but you will still not be free. And there are those of you who are here, and you are free. I want to say to you this morning, who are not incarcerated, behind walls, many of us find ourselves incarcerated to many other things. Gandhi says, "Freedom is a state, a mental state, of the mind." I would add to Gandhi's statement, freedom is a mental state expressing itself in spirituality.

I. Christ's Grace Is Freedom

We can be socially free, but personally and inwardly locked up, bound like slaves. In Galatians, the entire theme of the book is the freedom of Christ. Paul starts out in the first chapter saying, "I am amazed that some of you who started in the freedom of Christ have now fallen away, and in doing so, you have fallen from grace. You have fallen out of grace and you are apostate, and in relationship to Christ, you are anathema. That is the word he uses, which is a strong Greek word, which means "cursed." You who have tried to justify yourselves and align yourselves with God through something other than grace, i.e., the law, you have alienated yourselves from God. You have become an apostate, and you are anathema, cursed. Our freedom is in Christ's grace. Our freedom is in the grace of God, given to us through what God did in Christ. It is so hard for us to grasp that, because we are so historically removed from those days. What Judaism had become in those days was ritual and law. They had 365 written laws about the one commandment "thou shall honor the Sabbath day and keep it holy." Three hundred and sixty-five expressions about that one law. When God's grace came in Christ, God's grace abolished, made anathema, all of that. We don't have to go back to that time to understand it. All we need to do is to take a close look at what takes place today.

II. Religious Rule-Keeping Is Bondage

My daughter was telling me about a church in Greenville that has been in the news recently and has made a big uproar. One of the things that the minister said was that they collected $50,000 and upward every Sunday. She was asking how they did that. I said, "I know a little bit about that." I'm not projecting on that church, but I know a little bit about that kind of situation. This is a statement I realize that's filled with many things, but they collect a group of people who obligate themselves to the law, and especially the law of tithing. The minister said the members gave 10–20% of their income every Sunday. There is nothing wrong with that, provided it is given out of love and grace. When it is given out of obligation, and when the minister is milking the guilt gland while preaching Old Testament law, then my Scripture tells me that kind of approach is a curse. That is not grace. That is religion that has obligated us with "shoulds and oughts." I want to say to you that God's grace came in Jesus Christ to set us free from the shoulds and from the oughts. I don't necessarily believe in tithing. Linda and I have given more than the tithe, but it is out of grace, out of love. It's not out of obligation. It's not out of ought. It's not out of guilt. Some of you this morning are here because you couldn't feel right today unless you've been in a worship service. You feel guilty if you don't worship somewhere on Sunday morning. You are in bondage. You are obligated by shoulds and oughts to the law. If you're not here this morning out of a sense of love and grace and joy and excitement, then you need to examine that. You need to look at it. We who preach oughtness and shoulds and obligations, according to the book of Galatians, should look very seriously at our motivation. Jesus Christ came to set us free. In that day the mark of that law was circumcision. And Paul says that if you come back and get circumcised, you are obligated to keep the whole law. Anytime you pick up one, you pick 'em all up. You can't pick up the law of the tithe and not pick up all of the dietary laws and everything else in the Old Testament. If you're going to be obligated by one, you're going to be obligated by all. Did Jesus come to abolish all that? No, He came to fulfill it. And how did He fulfill it? He fulfilled it in grace, God's unmerited favor. Paul says in this passage, you have been set free. Do not obligate yourselves again to the law. Do you have any idea what would take place in our churches if that were the basic essential message that people heard week after week after week? That God has set us free . . . free from sin, free from guilt, free from shame, free from the obligation of ought and should. That God has called us to live in the joyous excitement of freedom. God enables us through God's indwelling Holy Spirit to set us free from the shackles of addiction, to set us free from the shackles of obsessiveness. God's spirit has come to set us free, joyously, enthusiastically free, but we continue to obligate ourselves with the shoulds and the oughts of the law. As I've said all summer, we're frightened to death of grace. Frightened to death of grace! But grace and faith are coupled together in a unique kind of way. We try to put shackles or restrictions around our people, we of the clergy, we who are denominational leaders.

Several years ago, I was showing a movie to our people in a Bible study on Presbyterianism when the minister said, "We are people of three books, the Bible, the Book of Confessions, and the Book of Order." And I stood up and cut him off. I said to the class, "THAT Presbyterian is a person of three books, but this group of Presbyterians is not a people of three books." I will not be obligated by books of order, or books of confessions. I live, or attempt to live, my life in the freedom and the liberty of the spirit as God has revealed it in the grace of Jesus Christ. I will not be shackled by anything else, not by the canons of the church, nor by the rules and regulations of the church. That's what Jesus Christ came to abolish in the very beginning, and that's what Jesus Christ strives to abolish today. Grace and freedom is not free.

Remember the old Kris Kristofferson song, "Me and Bobbie McGee?"

"Freedom's just another word for nothing left to loose. Nothing ain't worth nothing if it ain't free."

Grace is not free. Freedom is not free. The freedom that God offers us in the grace of Christ is not free. It cost God everything in Christ.

Maya Angelou, in a book entitled *The Heart of A Woman*, writes about a slave named Tom. This particular slave worked hard for his master. So hard that in fact the master gives him permission to work after hours. After he put a good day in for the master, he walked to town and worked for other people for pay. He had done this for years. He had saved every dime that he had ever made. After many years of this kind of schedule, he goes to the master and says, "Boss, how much do a slave cost?"

The boss says, "Well, a thousand to twelve hundred dollars, but Tom, you're old. You'd be worth about six hundred."

Tom had saved about a thousand dollars. He went back to the cabin, and he slept on it, thought about it, and he came back to his boss and said, "Boss, freedom is a yet bit costly. I'm gonna wait 'til it gets a little bit cheaper."

Freedom is not cheap. Freedom cost God. Jesus Christ was nailed on a horrible cross and died in an excruciating, humiliating death. There is the cost of your freedom and my freedom. There is the cost. God paid the price that we might be free . . . internally free. Free from our sins, free from our guilt and the shame of that sin, and free from the shackles of whatever addiction and obsession might capture and contain our minds or our physical desires.

III. Grace, Faith, and Love Are All That Count

Hear what Paul says in the 13th verse of this chapter: "You, my brothers were called to be free, but do not use your freedom in indulging your sinful nature—rather, serve one another in love. You are free." This is a one-word fulfillment, the Scriptures call it. For all the law is filled in one word. Even this, "thou shalt love thy neighbor as thyself." It is the royal law of James. "If you fulfill the royal law, according to the Scripture, 'thou shalt love thy neighbor as thyself,' you do well." It is the new commandment of the 13th chapter of the Gospel of John, "a new commandment I give you, that you love one another as I have loved you."

Jesus summed it all up this way in the 12th chapter of Mark and the 22nd chapter of Matthew. Jesus said, "Thou shalt love the Lord thy God with all thy heart, with all thy soul, and with all thy mind and strength." And the second is this, "Thou shalt love thy neighbor as thyself." You know what Jesus was saying in those words? All of the obligation of law is summed up in this, you are to love the Lord your God with all that you are, and I want to tell you how to do that. You love God through loving your neighbor as yourself. I don't know how to worship God. I do not know how to love God in any other way than loving the likes of you, and you, and you. I don't know any other way to do it. We are the recipients of grace, God's unmerited favor, to be grace. We are the receptors of grace, to be the recyclers of grace. We receive this kind of unmerited, undeserved love from God for one reason, that we might be the love of God on this planet. We are the recipients of God's grace for one reason, that we might be grace to other people . . . that we might be gracious in our relationships to other people, that we might be grace, unmerited and undeserved, forgiveness of others, unmerited and undeserved kindness to others, unmerited and undeserved care of others. That's what this is all about. It's not rules and regulations. It's not ritual and sacrimony. It is about love. Love expressing itself to each other in grace. And just like the Jewish people of old, as they forgot that, we have forgotten it.

Our churches are not institutions of freedom and liberty. Our worship is not expression of liberty and freedom. We write out a bulletin, and it is as if that bulletin were written by the hand of God. We better not deviate from it. You come to my church, we won't. I'd love for them to. Brother Gene Ghent said, "You've never heard Gene Rollins preach 'til you've heard him preach to a black congregation." And he's right,

I'll have a time at the prison on September 30th. They talk back to me. That's just like saying "sic 'em" to a dog. We have a great time. I relish the freedom in that, and I realize we white folk can't do that. We're not like that. That's not part of who we are and what we are. But we need not feel so bound and restricted by our liturgies of worship and by the way we approach worship and religious life. We approach it that way. I ought to do this . . . I should do that . . . I must do this. Where's liberty? Where's freedom? Where's the grace to be different and to be who you are? We structure little churches that respond and apply to this particular group of socioeconomic people. This particular group of socioeconomic people will fit in well to our church, so we invite you to come on over. Where's the liberty and where's the freedom to be who we are in our religious worship? And to be who we are in expressing God's grace and God's love. Yes, Christ came to set us free. Paul says stand in that freedom. Do not give it up. Do not allow it to be taken away. Stand firm in that freedom.

Conclusion

We are very much like that old ship that was hauling black ivory from the African coast. It had 200 black expressions of that ivory, called slaves. Aboard this particular ship, according to E. P. Dickey, there was an African Chieftain who was willing to die rather than be a slave. He plotted and planned and waited for the right moment, and it came. They broke free, overtook the ship, killed all of the crew and threw them overboard. They cried out, "We are free." Then they realized, free to do what. We don't know how to operate this thing. They looked at the compass, and they remembered that the sailors looked at the compass devotedly. So they thought it was some kind of God, and they worshiped it. They bowed down to it, and prayed to it, all to no avail. They were free, but without a compass. Free, but without direction. Free, but without power. We're not like that. We have been set free and given the compass of the Holy Spirit to live within us, to direct us, to guide us, and lead us into greater freedom and greater liberty. We have been set free internally. We have been the recipients of God's awesome love and God's awesome grace.

God has said you now are responsible one way. That's all, one way. You've been graced to be grace. You've been loved to be love. You've been forgiven to forgive. Throw out everything else and live your life graciously, receiving my grace and being my grace. Throw everything else out, live your life receiving my love and loving others. Throw everything else out, receive my forgiveness and forgive others. Sounds simple doesn't it? How can we mess up something so simple? We've done it. We continue to do it.

Stand firm, Paul says, in your grace, for grace has set you free. Do not return again to bondage. Whatever your bondage may be, God in Christ wants you free of whatever your bondage is.

Let us pray: Oh, Lord, there are those here this morning who are in just as much bondage as those I will be preaching to on September 30th. There are those here whose freedom is just as restricted as their freedom is. There are those here bound with shoulds and oughts, ill feeling and bitterness toward others, unforgivenness abounding and binding. There are those living out their obsession, living out their addictions, without power and without freedom. Let us hear your word today. You have come to set us free. Stand, therefore, in that freedom, and do not return again into the bondage of slavery. Oh God, set us free to be recipients of your grace. Help us to truly believe we are graced to be grace. May it be so, in Jesus' name. Amen.

❧ Chapter Sixteen ❧

Grace! It's Sufficient

TEXT: 2 Corinthians 12:7–10

CIT: Paul was a child of God who had a pain in his life that wrung from his heart the intense prayer that the Lord would remove it, but God did not.

THESIS: Through the sufficiency of God's grace, the "thorn-room" is an essential station on the way to the "throne-room."

PURPOSE: *Major objective:* supportive

Specific objective: Through the power of the Holy Spirit, I hope to lead each of us in trusting the sufficiency of God's grace.

TITLE: "GRACE! IT'S SUFFICIENT"

INTRODUCTION

OUTLINE:

I. The Thorns of Life—v. 7

II. Do the Thorns Remain Because of the Lack of Faith?—v. 8

III. Do the Thorns Remain Because of Unconfessed Sin?—v. 8

IV. The Thorns Remain to Prove the Sufficiency of God's Grace—vv. 9–10

CONCLUSION

Dr. Eugene C. Rollins

Scripture Reading: 2 Corinthians 12:7–10

To keep me from becoming conceited because of these surpassingly great revelations, there was given to me a thorn in my flesh—a messenger of Satan to torment me. Three times I pleaded with the Lord to take it away from me, but He said to me, "My grace is sufficient for you, for my power is made perfect in weakness." Therefore, I will boast all the more gladly about my weaknesses so that Christ's power may rest on me. That is why for Christ's sake, I delight in weaknesses, in insults, in hardships, in persecutions, in difficulties. For when I am weak, I am strong.

Introduction

This is a wonderful crowd to close out the summer of 2001. It has been a marvelous summer for me. I always approach this Sunday as a little bittersweet. You know, bitter that it's over, for a lot of you I won't see again until next year. Then sweet because it is over. I'm experiencing mostly bitter this year. It's been a good series for me. I have thoroughly enjoyed preparing it and sharing it with you, and hope the Lord has blessed you and touched your life through the Scriptures and the singing and just the fellowship together. I hope grace has taken on a new meaning for you. For those of you that were up before daylight, you experienced with me another expression of natural grace. The moon just hung out over the lake like a darkened sunset. It was just absolutely gorgeous this morning. I hope you found a new term for those kinds of experiences. It is a natural expression on God's grace to us. I'm accused at times by some of our people at the church of not believing in miracles. I have a different term for that. They're acts of grace. Acts of grace. So when your life is touched by the smile of the child, by a touch of a lover's hand, a good night's rest, or burping after a good meal, it is an act of grace—where you have been the recipient of goodness and mercy. It has been an act of grace to be with you this summer. You know, I could come down here and preach to the trees, and I have done that. Not necessarily here, but I've done that. It's an act of grace to be able to have you sharing with me as your part of our worship together. It is a delight to be with you. If you were not aware of our meal, please stay. We have plenty. Our cooks have been busy since very early this morning. Each Sunday, I just show up and preach. I don't do anything else. Jim Hudson, let's give him a hand, has been marvelous working our sound system all summer. We have had a great summer, as far as the sound system is concerned. No problems at all. For all of those who park the people and give out bulletins, and Jim also cuts the grass, and all of the others who work all summer and prepared the meal this morning, let's give'em a great big hand of appreciation. One other word of announcement. We are celebrating our 150th anniversary at Liberty Hill the entire month of October [2001]. The last Sunday in October, we are having dinner on the grounds. We've ordered a big tent and all that. I realize we have a crowd this morning because we are feeding you. We'd like to feed you again, the last Sunday in October. Come on up to the Hill, and be with us, as we conclude our 150th anniversary celebration that last Sunday of October. For those of you who have churches, we are not in the business of proselytizing. We want you to return to the church that you belong to and the church that you are a part of, but for those of you who do not have church homes and you come to the lakeside because you know the ceiling won't fall in, because there is no ceiling, come on up to the Hill. I'll assure you the ceiling won't fall on you up there either. So if you do not have a church home, consider coming on up to the Hill and joining us, as we worship the Lord every Sunday at 9:00 and 11:00. Again, welcome and God bless you for worshiping with us throughout this summer.

I. The Thorns of Life

Our text is the magnificent 12th chapter of 2 Corinthians. I really should read it all and deal with it ALL, but for time's sake, we will just look at the last half of it. But it really should be considered as a whole, and I will mention the whole. We'll begin our reading with verse 7. [Scripture passage read.]

Were it not for this chapter, we would get the wrong impression of Paul. We would get the impression that Paul is always and constantly an overcomer. For you see, he was beaten on at least three occasions, and survived. He was stoned and left outside of Lystra for dead, and survived. He was shipwrecked, and for three days and nights was tossed about on the sea, and survived. Survived only to go ashore and was gathering wood for a fire for the survivors, and he was bitten by an Asian pit viper, and survived. He was imprisoned on three different occasions and he wrote some of his most courageous, marvelous work, such as Philippians, while he was in prison. Were it not for this chapter we would say Paul is one of those special untouchable folks. So radiant in the face of sufferings, I cannot feel any kinship to him at all, were it not for this chapter. In the beginning of this chapter, Paul lays out for us, I think, the sights of heaven and then talks about the stresses of life. That's the latter part of the chapter we looked at. But in those sights of heaven, at some point in his life, he possibly had a near death experience and saw the radiance and glory of heaven. We don't know when that took place. A lot of questions are in this chapter. There are those that are convinced that when he fell blind, and was blind for three days after that Damascus meeting with Jesus, he had his spiritual eyes opened, and he saw these magnificently, heavenly visions. It may be.

Others believe it was while he went to Arabia on Mt. Sinai after his conversion experience. After our own conversion, if we are going into the ministry, most of us go into seminary. Paul didn't go to seminary. He went to Arabia for three years and sat at the feet of Jesus, according to his testimony. I remember fussing about it taking three years to get a master's degree in divinity. That's absolutely ridiculous. I don't know of any other discipline that takes 98 semester hours to get a master's degree. And I said, "Why?" They said, "Well, Paul went for three years." Duh! Anyway, while Paul was on Mt. Sinai, there are those who say that it was there that he saw all these heavenly visions. It may be.

There are still others who, like that 14th chapter of Acts, when he was stoned outside of Lystra, say he was stoned and left for dead. It was that time when he experienced this near death experience and saw the wonders and glories of heaven. That well may be. We don't know. Paul talks about these special revelations, and we don't know what they were, nor when he received them. In the midst of that, he says, "Unless I be overly puffed up, unless I become arrogant, there was given to me a thorn in the flesh." That's another possibility of uncertainty in this chapter. We don't know what the thorn was. In the Greek it is "steakos," which means "a stake." A stake that was driven painfully in Paul's life. We don't know what that stake was.

John Calvin, the Presbyterian founding father, was convinced that it was a spiritual struggle. It was a spiritual temptation. And Calvin quoted the fact that Paul was consenting to Stephen's death, the first deacon. It is that spiritual struggle Paul never got over. Well, I'm not as convinced as Calvin was.

Luther, the founder of Lutherism or the founder of the Lutheran Church, believed that it was the Judaizers who followed him around trying to correct the gospel message, and it was that kind of persecution that Paul was talking about with the thorn. I don't know.

The Roman Catholic Church believed, and still continues to believe, that Paul's thorn in the flesh was his carnal desires, his fleshly desires. Because of some of the language about women in Paul's writings there . . . and this is a Roman Catholic Church belief, that either Paul was married and wanted not to be or he was not married and wanted to be, and that he had these awesome struggles with women. Well, maybe. Maybe not. We do not know what the thorn was, and I believe we do not know what it was for a reason. And that is, no matter what our thorns are, we can identify with Paul's thorn.

Paul was inflicted with something that would not go away. There are those who believe, and this is where I am, that in Paul's travels he came down with malaria. Because malaria in that day was a continuous disease that was incurable, it brought about eye weakness, and we do know from Paul's writings that his eyes were weak. We have a hint in his writings that he may have had some type of seizures from time to time. All of this is consistent with malaria, untreated. And then there are those who say no, his thorn was his small stature, his unimpressive size, and his unimpressive speech. Well, we don't really know what it was, and in not knowing what it was, we can better identify with the fact that here is a person who struggled with something in his life, and he asked God on numerous occasions. Don't fundamentalize the three. That's the way a Hebrew thinks. "Thrice," the Old King James says. Three times Paul prayed. Well, in the Hebrew understanding that was continuous, not just three times. But Paul prayed time and time again that this thorn would be lifted from him, that this, whatever it was in his life, would be taken away, but it never was. He never was relieved of this thorn in his life. And I believe that helps us to know that God is not necessarily in the thorn removing business. That's not exactly God's job description. But there are times when all of us are confronted with issues and hardships and it simply will not go away. It will not be changed. It will not be healed. It will not be lifted. And we are going to be involved in that thorn, whatever it might be, apparently from now on.

II. Do the Thorns Remain Because of Lack of Faith?

I want to correct and speak to two approaches to this that I find deeply, deeply discouraging, painful, and hurtful. Do the thorns of life remain because our faith is not strong enough in God to remove them? I want to say an emphatic NO to that. Thorns, sicknesses, handicaps, troubles, trials, whatever they may be, do not remain because we do not have the faith to have them removed. Do you know anyone who had more faith than the apostle Paul? Do you know anyone who demonstrated more faith than the apostle Paul? Finally, after three imprisonments, he died as a prisoner to the guillotine. Faithful unto death. Was Paul's thorn removed? No! No! Did he have faith? Absolutely! And I believe when we listen to these TV evangelists and radio evangelists and a lot of others who talk about "if you just have faith, if your faith is strong enough, this is going to be taken from you." They quote all kinds of passages in the Scripture. They live what I call the "abundant life syndrome"—that if you just have faith, life is just going to be absolutely abundant, and you are going to be victorious over anything and everything in your life, if you just have faith. I want to say to you, that is not biblical.

The apostle Paul lived under the hardship of a stake in his life until death. And it was not removed. And he asked for it to be removed. And he asked in faith for it to be removed. I could cite you until well into the afternoon experiences of hurt and devastation in and around this misunderstanding. I'll only use one. I could use fifty at least.

He leaves early in the morning, as is his custom has been much of his life, before daylight. He picks up the newspaper, carries it back into the house, puts it on the cabinet just inside the door for his wife to read when she gets up, and he goes back to his car, gets in his car, and goes to work. That's been his habit for years. He goes out and picks up the newspaper, and as he reaches over to pick up the newspaper, he is hit from behind by an assailant, beaten severely around the head. His wallet is taken. His watch and rings are taken. When his wife wakes up and does not find the paper in its normal spot, she opens the door and finds him lying on the lawn in a pool of blood. Seventeen years later, she is taking care of a husband, who has not recognized her since the night before the assailant beat him about the head. Seventeen years, she has been lovingly caring for a man who has been beaten so severely that his mental recognition never returned. Then he took pneumonia and died. A dear sister, from her Bible study, said to her, "Do you not know that if you'd just had the faith, he would have been healed years ago." I cannot begin to tell you how devastated that woman was. This dear saint, who has cared for an invalid husband seventeen years, was told by someone whom she respects and significantly believes that if her faith had been sufficient, he would have been healed. Stories like that I heard constantly up and down the halls at Richland Memorial Hospital as a chaplain. I want to say to you, why then was Paul's thorn not removed? He had ample faith, more than ample faith, and died with his thorn.

III. Do the Thorns Remain Because of Unconfessed Sin?

There are those who like to quote that verse in Psalms, "If I regard inequity in my heart, the Lord will not hear my prayer." This thorn remains in my life because of unconfessed sin. Was there unconfessed sin in Paul's life? Was there sin that kept him from being healed of this thorn? There is no indication of that. None whatsoever. None. If that were true, not any of us would ever have any kind of thorn removed from our lives. For the Scriptures tell us to break one law is to be guilty of them all. If we think it in our hearts, so it is. We cannot get beyond the first commandment. The first commandment says, "Thou shalt love the Lord thy God with all thy heart, soul, mind, and strength." If you're able to do that, please remain after the service and talk to me. I want to know how you do that. I need your help. So there is none of us without sin. Not any. We're guilty because of what we do. We're guilty because we think it in our hearts.

IV. The Thorns Remain to Prove the Sufficiency of God's Grace

And then the Scripture says, "To him that knoweth to do and doeth it not, to him it is sin." Do you know some good that you're not doing? Hello. Do you? Do you know some good things you're not doing? You've made every visit that God's ever put on your heart and mind? You've given every dime you've thought about giving? You've done everything you've thought good to do? Come on now. We're all guilty, and there's where the grace of God comes in. It is the grace of God; God's unmerited, undeserved forgiveness of us. So these thorns in our lives are for what purpose? Why do they remain? Why was Paul's thorn left? We read it. Paul said, God said to me, "No, I'm not removing your thorn, because I want you to see. I want you to know experientially. I want you to know every day of your life that my grace is sufficient. My grace is sufficient." No matter what your handicap, no matter what your issue, no matter what your thorn, no matter what your stake, God's word says "my grace for you will be sufficient." You do not have to give in. You do not have to succumb. You do not have to live victimized. My grace is sufficient.

Paul said I'm not just going to survive then, I will boast of my weaknesses. I will boast of my hardships, I will boast of my trials because in these trials, in these hardships, in these weaknesses, God's strength is going to be made perfect. In my weakness, I acknowledge God's strength, and in my weakness, I find God's grace to be sufficient.

What a way to live. Believing that no matter what I face, no matter what trial, no matter what hardship, no matter what difficulty, God is going to be with me, and God's care and grace toward me is going to be absolutely, finally sufficient. I do not have to live failing. I do not have to live as a victim. God's grace is, and will be, sufficient.

Conclusion

I was reading some notes from a diary that was found in 1995 and published. The name of the person was Edie Ethie Hillsome. She was a young Jewish woman in Amsterdam, Holland, when the Nazis took over and started gathering the Jewish people for the Holocaust. Like all of her friends and family, she hid out. She disguised her ethnicity and prayed and prayed and prayed for the salvation of Holland, for the relief of Nazi terrorism. Riding a bicycle in November 1941, she came to the realization that she was going to live her faith every day in the open, and she was going to believe that God's grace would be sufficient for her. And while her life was becoming more and more terrible externally, her inward life was blooming like a rose and continued to do so until November 1943, when she was led into the gas chambers. Preacher, is that victorious? Is that sufficient grace? Yes, it is. Yes, it is. It is sufficient grace to face death knowing this is not the end. It is sufficient grace to face this kind of horrible situation externally when internally you know that you are victorious, and that's what Paul was saying.

Neither death nor life can separate me from this sufficient grace is what he was saying. What a difference our lives would take on if we truly believed deep within us that whatever this hardship that I'm having to face, whatever this change, whatever this transition that I'm moving into, God's grace is going to be sufficient. Whatever I have to deal with, God's grace is going to be sufficient for this moment in time, for this thorn in my life. For you see I truly believe that the thorn room we spend so much time in is necessary to prepare us for the throne room where we will one day know as we are known, see as we are seen, and all the thorns of our lives will make sense, as we view them in the context of God's overall grace and care for us.

Between now and the first Sunday of June next year some of you that are in the sound of my voice will not be back with us next summer. You'll not be with us again. You'll go on to glory. There are those of you here who cannot even imagine the kind of hardship that you're going to be faced with before next June. I want to say to all of us, no matter what I have to face between now and when we see each other again, no matter what you have to face, no matter what thorn comes into our lives, God's grace is going to be sufficient, for you, for you, for you, and for you, and for me. Paul concluded, "God's strength is made perfect in my weakness," and may it be so for you and for me.

Let us pray: Oh, Lord, your undeserved, unmerited favor we know as grace, may it truly be sufficient for each of us today and the days ahead. We thank you that we do not know what we'll have to face. We do not know the future, but help us through our faith to truly believe in who holds the future, and to believe before the future's entered into, your grace is sufficient for us all. In Jesus' name. Amen.

✁ *Notes* ✁

[1]. Brown, H. C., H. Gordon Clinard, and Jesse Northcutt. *Steps to the Sermon.* Nashville, TN: Broadman Press, 1963.

[2]. Sloek, Johannes. *Devotional Language.* Berlin and New York: de Gruyter, 1996, pp. 53–96.

[3]. Armstrong, Karen. *The Battle for God.* New York: Alfred A. Knopf, 2000.

[4]. Spong, John Shelby. *A New Christianity for a New World.* New York: Harper Collins Publishers, 2001.

[5]. Brown et al., p. 98.

[6]. Arberry, A. J. *The Koran Interpreted.* New York: Touchstone, 1955 (p. 45, "The Cow").

[7]. Armstrong, p. 56.

[8]. Ore, Nancy. *You Are Enough! A Woman Seminarian's Story.* Rosemary Radford Ruether, Womanguides.

[9]. Camus, Albert. *The Fall.* New York: Vintage Books, 1956.

[10]. Smedes, Lewis B. *Shame and Grace.* San Francisco: Zondervan Publishing House, 1993, p. 111.

11. Sample, Albert Race. *Racehoss: Big Emma's Boy.* Austin, TX: Eakin Press, 1984.

12. Hemingway, Ernest. "The Capital of the World." In *The Short Stories of Ernest Heningway.* New York: Scribner, 1953, p. 38.

13. Smedes, p. 37.

14. Campbell, Will D. *Brother to a Dragonfly.* New York: The Seabury, 1977, pp. 220–224.

15. Boys, Mary C. *Has God Only One Blessing?* New York: Paulist Press, 2000.

16. Smedes, pp. 23–25.

17. Hugo, Victor. *Les Miserables.* New York: Penguin, 1976, p. 111.

ᗌ Selected Bibliography ᗏ

All Scriptures used are from the New International Version, 1978.

If only one or two books could be read along with this study, I would recommend the following:

1.   Lewis B. Smedes. *Shame and Grace.* San Francisco: Zondervan Publishing House, 1993.

2.   Philip Yancey. *What's So Amazing About Grace?* Grand Rapids, MI: Zondervan Publishing House, 1997.

3.   James Montgomery Boice. *Whatever Happened to the Gospel of Grace?* Wheaton, IL: Crossway Books, 2001.

4.   Matthew Fox and Rupert Sheldrake. *Natural Grace.* New York: Doubleday, 1997.

5.   Charlene Spretnak. *States of Grace.* San Francisco: Harper Collins Publishers, 1991.

Index